DAMP

THE ULTIMATE GUIDE TO **MINDFUL DRINKING HABITS**
AND **CUTTING BACK FOR GOOD**

Jean Crissien

Jack-Devil Media

Title: Damp: The Ultimate Guide to Mindful Drinking Habits (and Cutting Back for Good) / Jean Crissien

Description: First Edition | Jack-Devil Media, 2024 | Includes bibliographical references.

Identifiers: ISBN 979-8-9904668-0-7 (ebook) | ISBN 979-8-9904668-1-4 (paperback)

Cover design by the team at 100 Covers.

Download the FREE resources!!

I sincerely want this process to end with a better you, which is why I created some critical tools to guide your progress.

Go the the book's hub at mindfuldrinkingbook.com to get:

1. The detailed **Workbook**
2. The **Serving Tracker** and **Goal Progress Spreadsheet**
3. The **Alcohol Habits Contract**

Contents

Introduction: Welcome to a Damp Lifestyle

"Here's to alcohol, the rose-colored glasses of life."

F. Scott Fitzgerald

At this moment, you're cracking the first page of a better life. I know, it's a tall statement. But it's sincere. There's no better way to describe the power to control your drinking. I'm glad you're here for the journey.

Mindful drinking isn't new. In fact, there are plenty of other books you could have chosen. It's possible this isn't your first.

> There are two main reasons mindful drinking has a history; 1) Because you're not alone; 2) Because it works. Many have been here before you, many will arrive after.

Mindfulness is one of many paths to moderation and a healthier relationship with alcohol. I'm going to show you why it works and how to do it.

Most of us have been drinking for decades. In 1999, almost half of American college students reported *at least* 1 binge in the previous month. Another 1 in 4 reported frequent binges. So if you're 40 and went to college, you've got almost 20 years' experience getting lit. If you started in high school like I did, you could collect a full pension. By now, alcohol is a close friend that proudly strolls into your social events, date nights, and even your house.

It's also likely you've tried to cut back before. If you had mixed results, you are, once again, not alone. Most of us have been able to pare down the servings here and there, only to spring back into old form. Dry January becomes wet February. A healthy spring turns into a drunken summer. These ebbs and flows are common.

I can say, with conviction, that you can turn the tide to make **mindful drinking the norm rather than the exception**. This is a liberating reality.

For most people, the desire to cut back usually stems from some mix of morning regrets and deeper health concerns, especially as they become more nagging with age. There was a time when you'd revel in the dark humor of a wild night. Or shrug off Thursday morning's hangover after checking the Uber fare. Eventually—and unfortunately—something happens that's both weird and inevitable: The steady creep of alcohol, with its destructive potential, becomes no laughing matter.

I know this reality well. You do, too. Otherwise, you'd be reading a riotous Chelsea Handler book instead of this one. That reality is why 1 in 3 drinkers want to drink less than they do today. And the older you get, the louder your body cries uncle. Telling it to shut up while you pound espresso isn't working like it used to.

To their credit, public health officials are rushing to educate us on the dangers of alcohol. This has made it much harder to wave off their stats on anxiety, cancer, and other comorbidities. And their cries are hitting closer to home as we learn more about alcohol's toll. Consider a few somber facts:

1. Alcohol misuse is the leading risk factor for **death** in the 15 to 49 age group.

2. Alcohol is the leading risk factor for **disease** in the 25 to 49 age group, and the second-leading risk factor in the 10 to 24 age group.

1. Alcohol is a known **carcinogen** that increases the risks of various cancers, including throat, colon, and breast.

2. Drinking is linked with high blood pressure, heart disease, and stroke.

3. Alcohol weakens the **immune system**, increasing your chances of being knocked down by viruses and other ailments.

Quick summary: alcohol bad for body.

Those are just the long-term, chronic problems. The short-term issues, which we feel often, are more familiar.

I'm talking here about the lack of energy.

The interrupted sleep.

The weight gain.

The sugar and calories.

The sagging skin.

The raccoon eyes.

The hangxiety.

The leaky gut.

The bloating.

The brain fog.

The worry and dread.

The lagging productivity.

The poor dating choices.

We know alcohol's fingerprints are all over this list.

I'll bet you're ready for some good news, so here's three pieces; First, you can minimize the risks of alcohol by changing the way you drink; Second, the power to wrestle back control is squarely in your hands. And third, you're reading a book that will help you do just that.

When I started this project, my goal was to help people realize why they drank and what the consequences were. I wanted to remind everyone that choosing to have a drink should be, as Professor David McNutt put it, an active pleasure rather than a reflex and habit. In short, I wanted to tell my story while teaching others to **stop drinking mindlessly and start drinking mindfully**.

You'll find that this takes a little work. Mindful drinking means carefully building habits of conscious reflection until they become routine.

On the front end, this means nixing habits of excess and understanding our drinking behaviors. On the back end, it entails rethinking our entire approach to drinking. How hard could that be?

I'm neither a flashy celebrity nor a famous TV doctor. But I have a story worth telling. It started in my pimple-stained teen years and eventually led to the same questions you have now. When those questions arose, I measured the joy of alcohol against the pain. I balanced its addictiveness with my self-control. And I learned the triggers that make me crave a drink—and how those triggers have changed with time.

This book is the product of that journey. It's how I put down the heavy baggage that alcohol burdened me with for so long. (Like I said, decades.) I hope you're ready to walk the same path with a clear mind and an open heart. Because if you're here, it's time to peel back, reassess, and change your relationship with alcohol.

A Quick Preview of Mindfulness

Mindfulness has become a trendy catch-all to describe everything from spiritual meditation to intentional screen breaks. At this point, it's a living term that changes according to the context. For our purposes, we'll prune it down to a single word: **awareness**.

There are 3 things you're going to become aware of throughout this journey: **triggers**, **feelings**, and **servings**. Put another way, you're going to become more attuned to *what* **makes you drink**, *why*, **and** *how much*.

> Mindfulness helps us control alcohol by shedding light on our triggers, feelings, and servings, which gives us the information we need to disrupt old habits and build healthier ones.

You're going to become conscious of your thoughts and emotions surrounding drinking. One of alcohol's superpowers is to make you into a mindless robot. All of us get there. We embrace libations without giving much thought to why. When we become aware of the why, we open a path to understanding and controlling our drinking. Sounds kinda out there. But it's a very practical process that entails shedding light on unconscious behaviors.

The most concrete thing we know about mindfulness is that it *works*.[1] (I'll dig into this more in Chapter 6.) Another thing we can be sure of is that it's not a one-size-fits-all approach. Mindfulness looks one way when it's about being present and entirely another when it's about alcohol cravings. And techniques that work for one person are utterly useless to another.

Despite the variation in methods and experiences, mindful practices consistently help people find solutions to all kinds of problems. In this book, we're going to combine the awareness of mindfulness with the science of habits. This approach will help you to better understand your drinking and give you the tools you need to trim your servings.

You've done me the honor of cracking open my book. The least I can do is pay it forward by being transparent about my history. Knowing my alcohol journey will help you understand where I'm coming from and where our stories overlap.

This isn't just a cheap ploy to buy your trust, although I'll admit that's part of it. But it's more about rustling your mind, in the hopes you'll think about your own relationship with alcohol, which is surely full of its own twists and turns.

I figure the beginning is a good a place to start, although I'll admit I had to think hard about where the beginning really was. From there, I'll gradually make my way to the crescendo, which are the events that drove me to moderate with mindfulness. If nothing more, my story will serve as a reminder that you're in good, even if slightly sullied company.

A Refrigerator Door Opens

Black Friday, 1992. That was the day I had my first run-in with alcohol, three months before my 13th birthday.

My single mother, in her eternal money struggle, was at one of her customer service jobs staving off tirades from people sick of their in-laws. Somewhere between *Saved by the Bell* and *Boy Meets World,* it dawned on me that Mom left half a Thanksgiving wine box in the fridge. Made sense—she was never great at finishing glasses, let alone boxes.

Up to that point, my alcohol history was limited to parent-sanctioned baby sips. But I was suddenly having my first legit alcohol craving.

I ambled to our fridge, which looked more like a prop from *Roseanne* than a working appliance. The original cream facade had long faded, leaving only brown discolorations and a tired, leaky seal that offered little resistance to a kid craving leftover cranberry sauce, much less white Zin.

I yanked the door open, leaned in, and pretended for the first time to understand what "velvety body" means. No need to keep reading—velvety body was all the convincing a pre-teen boy needed. One thing was obvious: baby sips left too much to the imagination. It was time to take my liver for its first field test.

Three hours and as many velvety glasses later, my big brother came home from his weed-smoking mischief to find that I had migrated to the bathroom floor to fight off the queasiness. I vaguely remember him laughing and kicking me, as one might expect from an older sibling. My listless response was enough to confirm suspicions of drunkenness.

There I laid, experiencing for the first time the dizzying lows of overdoing it. And yet, until my mom walked in, I don't think I wiped a shit-eating grin off my face. Drunkenness was like kisses and carnival rides—nothing like the first time.

I never threw up that day (hold your applause), which meant that I shared the drinkers' genetic profile so common in my Colombian family. At 12, I knew nothing about genetic predispositions. But I've since learned that my DNA leans nicely into alcohol's euphoria while (mostly) skipping the nausea. Turned out I was a chosen one, ripe with potential to become the Michael Phelps of collegiate beer pong.

Thankfully, I wouldn't get to use my superpowers again for a while—rogue wine boxes appeared about as often as leap year. But I neither forgot the hints of plum nor the mind-bending potential of fermented grapes. I also didn't know how prominent alcohol would become in my life. But I'd find out soon enough.

A Socialite is Born

Turns out, against all odds, that Franzia is a gateway box.

The relationship that germinated at age 12 sprouted when I discovered house parties in high school. By junior year, I had blossomed into a seasoned party kid, getting a second education on proper keg tapping and beer bong science. Senior year ushered in the era of older sibling IDs and urban drive-thru liquor stores. That was how my high school days passed through the hourglass: plenty of substances with little substance.

By the time I moved to Flagstaff to do my bachelor's, I had a refined palette, knowing damned well that Boone's Farm was trash and decent folks drank Natty Light. This kicked off the era of trendy mixers, layered shots, and chasers—lots of orders with "bomb" at the end. I even prioritized social drinking by getting into Greek life, which I've since described as "a great community service opportunity." (Humble brag alert: My second priority was to graduate Magna Cum Laude, which I did. This is a damning indictment of American higher education.)

By now, you're getting the point—drinking was a "me" thing. Or, truer to life, a "we" thing. Since adolescence, alcohol has been laced into my social settings, friendships, family gatherings, and home life.

My friends and I labeled it "social drinking." But it was more than that. Binges, drunk weekends, all-day parties, "hair of the dog" mornings—all passed off as youthful fancy. It was how we, the fun-loving 18-to-25 demographic, tied our child-free lives together. The dicey situations we'd find ourselves in became fodder for epic tales rather than cautionary ones. The laughter was riotous. The hugs were exuberant. The victory laps were Olympic. And hangovers seemed like an old person's problem. (This last one is painfully true.)

Of course, I'm not the first person to have meshed high-risk drinking with higher education. It's a common method of social lubrication on college campuses. I'd even say it's a natural extension of American and European drinking cultures. Throughout our lives, we are pelted with alcohol messages. Most of them tell us that drinking is cool and alcohol makes everything better. Makes sense that young people adopt these rites of passage when it's their turn.

A bigger problem surfaces when college-style binges continue after graduation. For me, that was when things started getting complicated.

Mr. Hyde Shows Up

Against good advice, I committed to becoming a professor toward the end of college. The fallout was more homework. A lot, actually. Anyone who's chased a PhD can tell you it's a pride-swallowing siege, with endless academic reading and constant technical writing. It's the work of the walking dead. The short-term reward is poverty. The long-term paybacks are depression, anxiety, and a narrow job market.

My cohort made the whole thing bearable by clinging to each other like staticky socks. We also clung to pints and bottles. This was my next version of social drinking, carousing with the fellow victims of academia. If the purpose was to create community and build bonds, it worked beautifully. We all connected, shared our longings for a previous life, and helped each other walk the path. It was a clear example of alcohol's social benefits.

The rise of professional stress caused a shift in my alcohol journey. First, it was the grueling exams, which amount to a sick hazing ritual. Then came the dissertation writing, which serves a purpose but divorces a human from their soul.

Your prize for clearing those hurdles is the academic job market, which is short on jobs and long on applicants. You end up being a "good fit" for a handful of *extremely* competitive jobs. Not snagging one means your six to eight years of work end with unemployment or, worse, a Panera apron.

That's when it got weird with alcohol. You know that moment when a purely physical relationship is exposed as a sham? It was like that. To deal with all of it—exams, dissertation writing, job market pressures—I drank. This wasn't social or light. I wasn't having drinks on dates. I wasn't even chatting up a stranger at a bar. I was anxious, possibly depressed, at home, and alone.

Alcohol was no longer part a social experience—it was medicine. My habit steadily grew more precarious. Each time I opened the file for my dissertation—*just* double-clicking on a Word document—required a glass of wine. I even mentioned the Yellow Tail vintners in my dissertation's acknowledgments. (*Yellow Tail.* That's how sad it got.)

The job part somehow worked out. But by then **I had cemented high-risk, heavy drinking habits.** And they didn't go away with gainful employment. They stuck just like the social habits did. Even if these new habits weren't destructive, they would prove unsustainable. It was only a matter of time before I'd have to deal with them. Otherwise, living a healthy and happy life would prove difficult.

Quitting Vs. Cutting

When I started contemplating my relationship with alcohol, I did what any good nerd would do: read. I took to Google and keyed in whatever words made sense—"cutting back on alcohol," "books on safer drinking," "moderate alcohol consumption," and so on.

I eventually came across a review of the "quit lit," a subgenre in the addiction literature that focuses on sobriety. Most quit lit authors shared a perception: drinking is a runaway train destined for alcoholism. Some even insisted that "light drinking" was actually "light alcoholism" masquerading as "safe drinking." The most common conclusion? The only escape was to quit altogether.

This was a tough theme for me to reconcile. I was pretty sure that one of my psych classes taught me that an addiction led to something destructive—job loss, broken relationships, sexual favors, that kinda thing. Didn't sound like me.

Long-tenured professor? Check.

Pedestrian-but-respectable credit score? Check.

Responsible parent? Two checks, one for each kid. (No third checks, thank you.)

I've been to enough performance reviews to know that checked boxes never lie. I was a pillar of adulting, with a smashing record of waking up and doing what I was supposed to.

I read on and felt **increasingly resistant** to the perspective that *all* **alcohol struggles are symptomatic of alcoholism**. By that standard, 30% of Americans have the disease. But to make sure I wasn't just telling myself what I wanted to hear, I kept digging.

More research took me to the clinical side of alcoholism, which added more perspective. The gist is that alcoholism is very real. The

American Society of Addiction Medicine, American College of Physi-
cians, American Hospital Association, American Public Health Association, and American Medical Association all concur. More agreement
comes from the American Psychiatric Association, American Psychological Association, and the National Association of Social Workers.

It's not just psychobabble—alcoholism is a chemical dependency
often linked to a genetic predisposition.

Unfortunately, the term is also vague and hard to diagnose. Doing so
accurately often requires openness from alcoholics themselves about
the personal impacts of their drinking. Once diagnosed, the clinical
term is "alcohol use disorder" (AUD), which runs on a spectrum from
mild to severe. The entire disorder is defined as "a medical condition
characterized by an impaired ability to stop or control alcohol use
despite adverse social, occupational, or health consequences.[2]"

I read this and quickly arrived at a conclusion: If I could avoid adverse
consequences and control my drinking, I was by definition *not* an alcoholic. Case closed. So freed was I from the shackles of alcoholism that
I opened a bottle of wine.

But the quit lit's fatalist tone left an impression. It made me wonder
whether my drinking was worse than I had admitted to myself. The
biggest issue, however, is that those authors were using a vague term to
describe *all* alcohol problems, regardless of consequences or genuine
attempts to cut back. Put another way, they were expressing how they
felt about alcohol, not its inevitable end point.

The truth, as I see it, is that you can feel like alcohol has become
problematic without resorting to labels or drastic self-diagnoses. Let me
be clear—this isn't a cheap shot across the bow of quit lit authors. They
write good books that help problem drinkers find clarity. It just felt like
they were written for someone else.

Drinking leads some people to excess and despair, and since they
can't control it, they quit. Good for them. What if I have the excess
without the despair? Better yet, **what if the excess can be cut out
entirely?**

I dug some more, eventually finding books that spoke to moderation, or what I call the "cut lit." These were usually written from a
clinical standpoint and read more like choose-your-own-adventure
books, guiding the reader until she found what suited her. The messages

weren't all self-affirming and cautions were everywhere, but they were more applicable to drinkers looking to cut back versus quit.

The cut lit introduced me to the **habit perspective,** which emphasizes **individual choices versus disease and addiction.** The unifying theme across these books is that drinking behaviors become embedded in our subconscious, largely thanks to alcohol's pharmacology. To fix that, we have to recondition ourselves by being intentional about our choices. Cut lit authors talk about cognitive behavioral therapy, spotting triggers, and seeing alcohol for the devious drug that it is.

Both the quit lit and cut lit had important lessons, as did other books from psychologists, clinicians, doctors, and academics. Building on all of it, I learned why moderation is as legitimate as abstention for *most* drinkers. In non-severe cases, it might even be better. In short, **controlled drinking is both possible *and* can have benefits.**

I want to be clear about the scope of this argument: I am not saying that addiction specialists, recovering alcoholics, or certain writers are wrong about alcoholism. For whatever reason—psychological, genetic, or otherwise—some people are best served by abstention. The slope is too slippery and their lives suffer, along with the lives of others.

I'm simply saying there's more than one way to skin the alcohol cat. Most of us are perfectly capable of controlling our intake and benefiting from the brighter side of alcohol. As Michael Levy wrote, the habit perspective "opens the door to the possibility that people can learn to drink differently."[3]

I can attest to the truth of Levy's message, namely that mindful habits *can* be learned. But there's no magic pill. It takes concentrated effort.

Does Moderation *Really* Work?

We've established that alcoholism is a real condition and that "alcoholic" doesn't describe all drinkers. In fact, it doesn't describe *most* people who drink. For that silent majority, cutting back is a perfectly legitimate alternative to quitting.

But does moderation really produce healthy results for people? As a matter of fact, in most cases, moderation leads to more success than abstention. Consider some facts:

- Clinicians say people who **aren't dependent** on alcohol **are well-suited for moderation.**[4] This is backed up with evidence.[5]

- These same practitioners emphasize that severe AUD is best treated with abstinence. This reiterates that one size *does not* fit all and some people are better off quitting.

- The National Longitudinal Alcohol Epidemiological Study (NLAES) found that **almost 60% of people** who *have not* been treated for alcohol misuse are successful at moderation.

- NLAES also found that **28% of those who *have* been treated** for misuse are successful at moderation.

- The strongest predictors of successful moderation are **motivation and confidence.**[6] If you *want* to change and don't have a dependence issue, you can probably moderate with mindful habits.

Again, the point here isn't to diminish the destructive power of alcoholism. It's simply to point out that moderation is legitimate *and* broadly successful. This is especially common in people without a physical dependence, non-daily drinkers, and those who have not had severe problems (e.g. losing jobs, poor work performance, legal troubles, etc.).

Don't doubt it for a second—moderation is absolutely possible for most drinkers. We just need to mobilize it effectively. And that's exactly what we're going to do in the chapters that follow.

Chapter Summary

- You can minimize the risks of alcohol by moderating your drinking. The **goal of this book** is to help you do that by building mindful drinking habits.

- Mindfulness is about **awareness**. Mindful drinking is about becoming aware of **3 things**: *what* makes you drink, *why*, and *how much*.

- For most drinkers, **cutting back** is a perfectly legitimate approach to addressing overdrinking. Quitting isn't the only path.

- The **habit perspective** advanced by cut lit authors focuses on individual choices versus disease/addiction.

- Cut lit authors have clearly shown that most drinkers are well-suited for **moderation**.

Chapter 1

Getting Started

Our Point of Departure

"Drink because you are happy, but never because you are miserable."

G. K. Chesterton

This book leans on a core principle: **we can manage alcohol, a powerful drug, with mindful habits**. The issue is that those drug properties are alluring. We go back repeatedly to chase the euphoria and relaxation, which are the brute force behind Big Alcohol's $1.5 trillion value.[1]

Unfortunately, those good feelings come with liabilities. Alcohol needles into our subconscious and lures us into excess. When that happens, alcohol becomes a foe rather than a friend. Once the costs have revealed themselves—*and* we're ready to listen—it's time to change the relationship.

No avid drinker wants to admit that the servings have taken a toll. The thought of our social world shifting from wet to dry makes us uneasy, like a Lexus owner faced with the prospect of taking the bus.

We lean on alcohol in social situations, plan wine country vacations, drink airport beers, and use it to kill stress. We struggle to imagine steak without wine or brunch without mimosas. We file "wine tours" and "beer tasting" in the Hobbies category.

Changing our drinking habits means experiencing life differently. It means thinking up new ways to do the things we do—or changing those things entirely. In the end, we squirm, we wince, we beg Bacchus to take a pinkie and leave the White Claw. But resistance, as the Borg say, is futile.

So here we are. Each of us has different motivations for changing, but they usually rhyme.

A doctor's wrinkled brow.

A parent shooting you glances at dinner.

Drunk-texting Dad instead of Deb, or Mom instead of Max.

A smashed scale whose only crime was accuracy.

A morning of hangover parenting.

A date that ended poorly.

A binge that turned into a lost day and a ruined week.

No reason is shameful, nor is any too big or too small. And sometimes, they come in numbers.

You're reading. That means you've taken a first step. Admitting you need to change is hard, even scary. Let's shed that fear by calling your relationship with alcohol what it is: **a problem in search of a solution**. Nothing more.

This doesn't make you an alcoholic or a bad person. You don't need an intervention. You're not on the cusp of marrying a second cousin. It just means you've gained some clarity about alcohol's risks and you're ready to find a compromise between soaking wet and bone dry.

Defining The Problem

The problem, neatly put, **is that drinking behaviors are positively reinforced habits**. In other words, we started a long time ago and keep doing it because it feels good. Over the years, we've conditioned our subconscious to believe that alcohol offers more reward than risk. We've also gotten stuck in patterns that feel automatic. My journey has taught me that untying these knots requires intentional *re*conditioning.

Over the last few years, I've learned that combining mindfulness with habit science is ideal for moderation. This is because drinkers usually drink without giving it a second thought. *That's* **what a habit**

is—something we do mindlessly, without thinking. It feels natural, like rinsing your hair after shampooing. Only in this case, we want to rinse without repeating so much.

My journey with alcohol took me to a place where I could no longer ignore the problem. I finally committed to addressing it for two reasons: family and health.

Tiny people came into my life. Not only are they precious, but they depend on me. Their arrival has given me new aspirations, like feeling spry enough at 60 to keep up with my youngest daughter. (She'll be 20. I've got my work cut out for me.)

I also wanted to max out my productivity so I could own more of my time. This demanded mental acuity, focus, quality sleep, healthy eating, and cardio. You know those nut jobs you see running at 5 AM? I'd have to be one of them. And if there are two things I hate, it's running and 5 AM.

In short, doing justice to the good fortune I'd had—both professional and personal—meant taking intentional steps to age gracefully and be better. And I knew those hopes would never take shape if I kept drinking at a weekly clip of 20 to 25 servings. Energetic, 5 AM people just don't do that, least of all in their 40s.

With time and effort, I put myself on a path to achieve those dreams. And I did so by successfully transforming my relationship with alcohol. By the standards of America's National Institute of Health (NIH), I went from being a "heavy" drinker to a "moderate" drinker. In some months, I slip down to "light" drinking. Taking extended breaks—like Dry January and Sober October—has steadily gotten easier.

To get there, I had to adopt mindful habits and focus on who I *really* wanted to be. It sounds like a climb, but it really wasn't that bad. And any work I put in has been entirely worth it. I think if you follow the path I've created, you'll find the same is true for you.

You have your own motivations for being here, which we'll dig into shortly. This book will help you reform your drinking habits so you can live better and longer. You'll get knowledge and tools that will help you live a damp lifestyle—not as wet as before, but not dry either.

To deliver on that promise, I'll give you high-quality information that will act as an in-depth guide to drinking habits, information that's backed by neurology, psychology, medical science, and more. I also include the experiences of clinicians who deal with alcohol problems daily.

In short, this book is a product of careful research and personal experience. I've also included practical tools to help you apply the knowledge you'll gain. Use them as you progress and then keep them close by for the future. Our relationship with alcohol is a living beast—if there's been excess in the past, there can be excess again later. But now you'll have resources to help you stay on top of it.

I do, however, want to be clear about **what you *won't* get: professional treatment for a severe alcohol problem.** If that's what you need, far better resources exist for you. That's also why we should make sure this book is for you before going any further.

Who This Book Is For

Damp is for avid drinkers who recognize that alcohol is a Janus-faced beast. Its benefits come with health issues and hangovers. The goal here is to control your drinking habits so that you can reap alcohol's rewards while minimizing its risks.

Most books in this space file all drinking problems under the umbrella of alcoholism, meaning that such problems will become progressively worse. I wrote this book for people who **reject that framing** for any of the following reasons:

- It doesn't reflect their experience with alcohol, which is more positive than negative.

- They recognize that most people drink, and the vast majority aren't alcoholics. Therefore, alcohol can't naturally cause this condition.

- They don't believe drinking is inherently good or bad—it can be both.

- They believe drinking patterns, in most cases, extend more from personal choices than genetics.

- They believe they can control their drinking by creating good habits.

Take your pick of reasons or plug in your own. It's okay to believe that alcoholism is a real problem *and* that your situation is different. By doing so, you're not belittling the struggles of alcoholics. You're not denying the affliction itself. You're just rejecting the idea that regular drinking wrangles you into the same diagnosis.

This book is also for people who **feel compelled to cut back** on alcohol because of the downsides. They might feel this for any of the following reasons:

- Age is changing their body's experience of alcohol—tougher hangovers, more fatigue, less mental clarity, more inflammation, etc.

- They've seen a recent spike in their consumption and are looking to take control. (This was a *very* common problem coming out of the Covid-19 pandemic.)

- Weight gain has become a problem, and they have pinpointed alcohol as a culprit.

- They've received medical advice to cut back (diagnosis, lab results, etc.).

- Life has changed, or they've taken on a new role. This includes marriage, parenthood, new jobs, etc.

- A loved one has commented on their drinking, causing them to reevaluate their relationship with alcohol.

- A bad experience has put a spotlight on their drinking. This includes accidents, legal trouble, or the results of other poor choices.

- They sense that alcohol has become a slippery slope and they need to wrestle back control. This includes too many binges, daily drinking, or "no off-switch" drinking.

- They fear that their current path puts them at risk of alcohol use disorder (AUD).

Damp is useful for big and small changes. You can cut your intake by half, by three-quarters, or by nine-tenths. You can aim for light drinking or moderate drinking. It's up to you. You're basically deciding **how much risk** you want to accept **in exchange for the benefits** of alcohol.

To guide your decision, I'll explain what alcohol does to your body and inform you of its consequences. Then I'll help you understand your drinking patterns and provide practical tips for cutting back. I'll also provide you with tools and exercises to help you along the way.

Who This Book Is NOT For

If you have any reason to believe you may have severe alcohol use disorder (AUD), this book is not intended for you. When people have severe AUD, it's likely because they were born with the genetic marker for alcoholism. This means it's probably chronic and potentially fatal. In such cases, successful moderation is *unlikely*.

> "If someone has the disease of alcoholism, drinking can't be consistently controlled. This loss of control is inevitable and largely defines the nature of the beast. No matter how hard you try, you have an inborn propensity to drink too much, and it will always be a challenge to control your drinking. So, the only way to avoid the problem is by never taking that first drink."
>
> Michael Levy, *Take Control of Your Drinking*, Chapter 2

Michael Levy wouldn't advise someone with severe AUD to use a book on moderation. Neither will I. I want to be clear on this point: While this book leans heavily on expert knowledge, it *is not* a replacement for professional treatment. If you have the notion that you should quit alcohol entirely, many wonderful books exist that are geared to that goal. I have included them in the resources section.

Awareness of severe AUD could come from a self-assessment or a professional evaluation. AUDIT has a quick self-assessment you can complete to give yourself an indicator of where you fall. Once you've given honest answers, it gives a risk score that puts you in 1 of 3 categories; low (0-7), medium (8-14), or high (15+).

If you land in the high range, AUDIT suggests you are likely to have a dependence issue. In those cases, *Damp* may not be the best book for you and professional treatment is likely a better option. Please understand there's no judgment here. I just want to make sure everyone gets to where they need to be.

With all of that said, if this book is for you, I hope you're ready to hear about my journey and apply it to yours. I'm over 40 and have children. If you're there with me, you might find eerie similarities between our lives. If we're in different places, that's okay. I think you'll still find my experience useful.

You and I share the common goal of improving our relationship with alcohol. If we succeed, we can keep it in our lives without taking on heavy risks. And there's a bonus: a better version of you is waiting on the other side.

How to Use This Book

The pages that follow are a guide to changing alcohol habits through mindfulness. You'll read about alcohol cravings, servings, habit science, and executing a mindful drinking plan. I'll tell you my personal moderation story along the way, which I hope will give life to the concepts. I've also included exercises and resources to help.

The **best way to use this book** is to approach it with an open mind while putting in time to do the exercises. There are 8 of them, which I hope sounds reasonable. (My professorial reflex is to assign homework, but I did my best to keep it light and breezy.) To make all of it easier, you can download the **free workbook** at the **book's hub**.

To change my drinking habits, I followed the **Stages of Change Model** commonly used by behavioral psychologists.[2] This means it was an iterative process that included **four stages**: contemplation, planning, execution, and maintenance.

I leaned on this model to organize the book into 4 parts:
- Part 1: Alcohol and Mindfulness, Explained

- Part 2: Getting Ready

- Part 3: Planning and Execution

- Part 4: Maintaining Mindful Habits

You'll notice that the parts are mostly a reflection of the stages of change model, with some background information up front in Part 1. I took some liberties in combining the planning and execution stages, mostly because they were so closely connected. I hope this structure smooths the bumps and helps you transition between one part of the process to another.

In Part 1, you'll get some background information on mindfulness, as well as alcohol's effects, risks, and benefits. What exactly are alcohol's effects on the brain and body? If alcohol is poison, why do we push forward with this ritual? Most importantly, why are alcohol habits so stubborn and why is mindfulness an effective approach for change?

Part 2 focuses on using mindfulness to become more aware of what alcohol does to your body and find the roots of your drinking habits. What are your triggers? Where did they come from? When does the "off switch" disappear and why? Then you'll learn about habit science and why it's a good approach for addressing the problem.

Part 3 digs into the practical side of living damp. This includes counting servings, dealing with cravings, and creating a positive environment. Then you'll put it all together to create and execute a plan: mindfulness, habit science, and practical tips for success.

Part 4 is about maintaining mindful habits in the long run. It might sound like an afterthought, but this last stage is especially important. To stay true to your goals, you have to maintain your new habits. This part covers how to tweak your identity, manage setbacks, stay motivated, and take on new challenges. It also discusses how to fill the space left behind by alcohol, which can be the hardest part of cementing moderation for the long run.

As with any self-help book, a lot of what's here will apply to you while some of it won't. Some exercises will meet you where you are, while others will feel too far ahead or behind. This is normal and expected. Just take what works and leave what doesn't. This is a self-directed approach to our problem, and there are many ways to win.

I know you're eager, so let's get started.

Chapter Summary

- **Core principle**: alcohol is an addictive drug, but we can manage it with mindful habits.

- **Main problem**: drinking behaviors are positively reinforced habits. **Habits** are behaviors you do automatically, without thinking.

- To change your drinking, you have to shed light on your **drinking habits**, so they are no longer automatic, mindless behaviors.

- This book is for avid drinkers who want to cut back for any variety of personal or health reasons.

- This book IS NOT intended for anyone who suspects they may have **severe Alcohol Use Disorder (AUD)**. It is not a replacement for professional treatment.

Part I: Alcohol and Mindfulness, Explained

Chapter 2

What Alcohol Does

The Highs and Lows of Drinking

"One tequila, two tequila, three tequila, floor."

George Carlin

There's a saying about aging that it's better than the alternative. This is meant to flip our perception, inviting us to celebrate getting older because it means we're not dead. What it also reveals is the double-edged nature of aging, namely that it's equal parts fortune and suffering.

Alcohol shares the duality of aging. All drinkers are happily aware of the highs, but these peaks sit in stark contrast to the lows. Both are products of a trick alcohol plays on our body. It manipulates feel-good chemicals first, then invites the come-down chemicals later.

The gap between up and down is big enough for alcohol to take credit for the former and little blame for the latter. By the time our hormones are out of whack, we don't even remember what we drank—or why. The insult to injury is that metabolizing alcohol wreaks even more havoc on our body.

It's good to know *why* all of this happens, because it builds a storyline of what brought us here. No matter who you are, no matter what you drink, your body feels both the highs and lows.

Why does one have to come with the other?

Why do we feel good when we drink, only to have hangxiety the next day?

Answering these questions now will help us make sense of the details that come later. We'll start with the good stuff—the highs—before moving on to the lows.

The High: Alcohol and the Pleasure Center

The familiar high you get from alcohol comes from the brain's **pleasure center,**[1] which includes parts of the brain stem, nucleus accumbens, ventral tegmental area (VTA), and amygdala. I know, I'm getting too deep into the biology of it. But it's important to understand that this brain wiring is largely responsible for desire, habits, and, potentially, addiction.[2]

In simple terms, **the pleasure center is what makes you *want* something.** (And want it again and again.) Alcohol teases the pleasure center by manipulating neurotransmitters, which are brain chemicals that fire messages across synapses (the gaps between neurons).

There are over 80 types of neurotransmitters at work in your brain, each of which you experience differently. Some, which we'll call uppers, turn up brain activity. Others, which we'll call downers, turn it down.

Alcohol affects two transmitters right away: dopamine and serotonin.[3] It goes like this: Moments after you raise a glass to your mouth, alcohol enters your bloodstream through your stomach. From there, it heads to your brain. Each sip is another "dose." And each dose triggers the release of dopamine from the nucleus accumbens, thus lighting up the pleasure center.

The ensuing gush of dopamine, which is both an upper and a downer, causes what's called "alcohol-induced euphoria"—the buzz we're so familiar with. You feel happy, gregarious, even better-looking. In the meantime, alcohol is also coaxing more serotonin, a downer, into your brain. This causes feelings of relaxation and mood enhancement.

Serotonin has long enjoyed the title of "feel-good" neurotransmitter. But it's also the first in a long line of downer chemicals released by alcohol. So while it's laughing at your jokes, it's also hatching a sinister plot to bring you down and kill the party. (More on that in a minute.)

Your brain quickly makes a positive connection between the dopamine-serotonin buzz and alcohol. This produces what's called "alcohol-seeking behavior," meaning that you'll go out of our way to get your hands on booze to get the reward again and again.

This "alcohol-reward" cycle is powerful enough to cement a drinking habit and is potentially addictive. And it all lies just underneath alcohol's crafty manipulation of the pleasure center.

Most of us can chase these rewards without slipping into the hole of addiction. But *none* of us can make repeated trips down the alcohol well without developing a strong attachment to it. The high is simply too powerful. On the other side of that high is the low, which quickly brings you back down to Earth.

The Low: Alcohol's Depressant Effects

It's an accepted medical fact that alcohol is a depressant. And yet, the dopamine-serotonin buzz tricks you into thinking it's a stimulant.

Think about it: You don't pour drinks at a party to slow things down, hoping that your guests will tire and leave. You do it to prod excitement and chatter—or to convince your date that you're the funniest Bumble match they've ever met.

Doesn't sound like a depressant, does it? And yet, alcohol goes from pseudo-stimulant to depressant by manipulating two more neurotransmitters: GABA (a downer) and glutamate (an upper).[4]

The short and skinny is that **alcohol's low comes from two simultaneous processes: glutamate suppression and GABA release.**[5] Together, these two neurotransmitters form the main on-off switch for the brain—glutamate turns it on, while GABA turns it off. Too much glutamate and you become overwrought and anxious. Too much GABA and you stop breathing.

When you're sober, GABA and glutamate are engaged in a delicate dance, balancing each other so you don't get too high or low. Alcohol shuts off the music and ends the dance.

First, it cranks up GABA. You start to feel relaxed, less anxious, and your inhibitions fade. This same process also shuts down the pre-frontal cortex (PFC), the part of the brain responsible for judgment and control. The door to bad decisions slowly creaks open.

Once you get to your second serving, alcohol starts to block your glutamate receptors. Now there's no upper to counterbalance the GABA, which can grind everything to a halt.

This shift in chemistry causes a gradual slowdown that becomes increasingly obvious. First, your breathing slows, and you become more sedate. Then your speech and movements become sluggish. Eventually, you start stumbling over chairs and butchering Beyoncé lyrics.

Unfortunately, the depressant effects of alcohol have negative consequences. Your nervous system reacts to the GABA release by cranking itself up, rushing stimulants into your blood to counteract the crash. Heightened nerves and stimulants produce—you guessed it—nervousness, stress, and anxiety. With time, this causes chronic cortisol spikes, among other issues.

The violent shift between depression and stimulation is especially noticeable the morning after, hence the notorious feelings of "drinker's remorse." The vague memory of telling your boss that performance reviews are stupid corporate fluff isn't helping the situation. (I mean, somebody had to tell him.) These regrets are exacerbated by post-alcohol anxiety, which is induced by a sensitive nervous system and overactive stimulants.

All drinkers are far too familiar with these effects.

For me, it wasn't uncommon for a five-day vacation to turn into a three-day funk. I used to think it was because I missed the beach. Now I know my body was still recovering from day-drinking on the beach. Then I'd order an airport beer, presumably to keep the good times rolling. But it was really to medicate the post-drinking anxiety by reintroducing alcohol to my system. Eventually, the only real fix is to ditch alcohol for a few days to get my body back to normal.

The whole thing stems from the push and pull that alcohol induces on your body, lifting you to soaring heights before carelessly yanking you back down. This happens, to some degree, *every* time you drink. They don't call it a drug for nothing.

As with any other drug, your body is charged with finding a way to metabolize alcohol and purge it from your system. Be thankful it finds a way. But don't go thinking that process is worry free.

The Effects of Metabolizing Alcohol

Your body uses digestive enzymes to break down alcohol until it becomes acetate, a harmless acid found in household vinegar. These enzymes metabolize alcohol by removing 3 hydrogen atoms, a process called **dehydrogenation**.

The problem is that this process is like burning fossil fuels and it produces pollutants that cause systemic damage. I don't want to get lost in biochemistry—or climate science, for that matter—but it's important to know that a toxic compound called **acetaldehyde** is the main byproduct of alcohol metabolism.[6] When your acetaldehyde footprint gets big enough, your body's environment is altered beyond repair.

To illustrate the details of alcohol metabolism over several drinks, let's go back to a place where multiple servings are the norm: college. *[Cue flashback sound effect...]*

You're back at your favorite bar, the one that drove a wedge between you and the dean's list. It's a Thursday, but you haven't been dumb enough to schedule a Friday class since the Psych 101 debacle. So it might as well be Mardi Gras.

A buzz waits for no coed, so you start with liquor, slipping a shot of tequila between some salt and a lime. A quick shudder and the night begins. Here's how the metabolism process starts:

- First up is an enzyme called *alcohol dehydrogenase* (ADH), which yanks two hydrogens. Your tequila briefly becomes **acetaldehyde**.

- Next up is *aldehyde dehydrogenase* (ALDH), which works quickly to remove the third hydrogen atom.

- Once that's done, acetaldehyde becomes acetate. Job done, yay body.

As this process happens, acetaldehyde starts leaking into your body's atmosphere. If you stop here, the damage won't be too bad.[7] But you just aced that biology test and "one-and-done" just won't do. (The same logic applies if you failed that biology test, so you're covered either way.)

As you walk back to the bar, the DJ fires up "This Is How We Do It" by Montell Jordan. Calendars and geography be damned, it's Friday night on the Westside. Time to rage, beer chasers all around.

After your second and third servings, ADH and ALDH are still on top of things. But their capacity is being tested. Instead of staying ahead of acetaldehyde emissions, they're only keeping pace.[8] Stop now and you're still okay. But the metabolism plot is poised to thicken.

At this point, dopamine, which is similar to cocaine, is flooding into your brain. Right at that moment, the DJ shifts the mood to Journey's "Don't Stop Believing." Everyone within earshot knows you love the high notes about holding on to that feeling.

Now on the verge of being discovered, you order a sugary concoction with a shot of Rumplemintz on the side. These represent your fourth and fifth servings and you're now officially in a binge. (That happened fast.)

Dehygrogenation continues at a feverish pace, but the drinks are too many and breaks too short. Here's a fresh update on your body:

- ADH and ALDH can't keep up. They call for reinforcements from backup enzymes.

- Backups pick up the slack, but they also produce new pollutants known as *reactive oxygen species* (ROS), a type of free radical.

- Acetaldehyde is spewing throughout your body and strains your environment. Ice caps are melting; seas are rising; Venice is on the brink of extinction.

For some reason—let's call it steely resolve—you pour on a 6th and 7th serving at the after party. At this point, your GABA levels are so high that your face looks like an Edward Munch painting. Gathering whatever motor skills you have left, you teeter over to an innocent stranger and annoy them with your favorite Che Guevara quotes.

The first time you fall, you pin it on phantom carpet sharks. The second time it's because "today was leg day." A semi-sober friend mercifully carries you to bed, helping you perform a convincing *Weekend at Bernie's* impression. The best news is that social media is in its infancy and your children won't suspect a thing.

[Cue end of flashback sound effect...]

Annnnnnnd, we're back. I know, it's bittersweet. Part of you wants to go full *Van Wilder* stay there forever. But, sadly, life goes on.

This is a good time to ruminate on something: how many similar episodes have you had throughout your life? (I couldn't possibly count mine.) That process took place in your body every time you drank with reckless abandon. And it didn't end there, as your liver kept laboring while you slept.

The biggest problem is that acetaldehyde, like most toxins, tries desperately to move in for good.[9] As if that wasn't enough, your body also experiences oxidative stress[10] and possibly even genetic mutations in cells.[11] All of this comes with serious risks, including cancer, which we'll discuss more in Chapter 5.

Previewing The Habit Connection

Our drinking story serves as a reminder that actions have bodily consequences. A single sip of alcohol is *mostly* harmless. But the steady amassing of drinks leaves a trail that heavily affects your quality of life down the road. As a society, we're becoming more aware of this. Hence the labels, warnings, and public service announcements.

Paying closer attention to our drinking is in vogue. But alcohol, being the tricky drug that it is, lures us into excess and makes moderation a struggle. In other words, it entices us with cravings and leads to unhealthy habits, simply because it prickles the pleasure center. But, like a wise guy in a gangster movie, it's all smiles until it shoots us in the back of the head.

As you begin to perceive alcohol as a drug-fueled habit, keep a few things in mind:

- Alcohol tricks our mind into thinking the good parts outweigh the bad parts. The truth, however, is that the **liabilities are equal to the benefits**. Possibly greater.

- The **reward effects** in the pleasure center are powerful—they effectively rewire parts of our brain. For some people, they're irresistible and potentially addictive.

- Over time, we build tolerance and **need more alcohol for the same rewards**. To compensate, **we drink more** and the risks multiply.

- When we drink frequently, it becomes a **chemically-reinforced habit.**

- Once formed, alcohol habits take **concentrated effort** to undo.

At this point, you're probably wondering how alcohol has survived human scrutiny for so long. Or natural selection, for that matter. If alcohol's so destructive, wouldn't evolution have weeded out the genetics of alcohol metabolism long ago? Why not rid homo sapiens once and for all of this anatomical wrecking crew?

The reason is that alcohol, believe it or not, has benefits. I'm not talking here about the dubious health advantages touted by Big Alcohol. I'm alluding to the neurological effects that stem from alcohol's psychoactive properties.

Basically, the same neurotransmitter dynamics we discussed above can do good things. Alcohol opens our minds, loosens our tongues, and tightens our bonds.

These effects make up the Dr. Jekyll side of this complicated drug, a collection of advantages that help explain alcohol's staying power throughout human history. We're going to zoom in on these benefits in Chapter 3 and Chapter 4. Before we get to that, let's do our first exercise.

Chapter Summary

- The high (AKA buzz) you get from alcohol comes from the way it teases the **pleasure center**, which happens through **neurotransmitters**.

- **Dopamine** and **serotonin** combine to give you the feelings of euphoria and relaxation (the high).

- **GABA** surges and **glutamine** suppression combine to produce alcohol's depressant effects (the low).

- This cocktail of neurotransmitters has lasting effects, including **anxiety**, **stress**, **nervousness**, and **hormonal swings** (especially cortisol).

- Alcohol metabolism (AKA **dehydrogenation**) produces toxic byproducts like **acetaldehyde**. It also produces free radicals, oxidative stress, and cell mutations.

- Our brain makes a strong connection between alcohol and the high, which is why we keep going back until we've solidified our **drinking habits.**

Exercise I

Exploring Binge Drinking

BACKGROUND: As you move toward mindful drinking, it's important to get an idea of the times, places, and faces that lead to overdrinking. I'll get into the specifics of consumption levels in Chapter 10. For now, we'll focus on **three definitions** from the National Institute of Health (NIH): [1]

- Heavy episodic drinking: 4+ drinks in a sitting (women) and 5+ drinks in a sitting (men).

- Binge: 4+ drinks (women) and 5+ drinks (men), within a 2 hour period.

- Extreme binge: 8+ drinks in a sitting (women) and 10+ drinks in a sitting (men).

In summary, we hit the threshold of high-intensity drinking at 4 or 5 drinks, depending on gender. The categories simply differ by time and volume. A binge, for example, is just heavy episodic drinking in a certain time frame (2 hours).

Details aside, the idea's the same across all 3 terms—we're drinking enough alcohol to get noticeably drunk *or more*. When we don't stop, it's commonly called "no off-switch" drinking.

As terms go, **heavy episodic drinking** is easily my favorite, as it nicely captures what binge drinking is all about: copious amounts of alcohol imbibed in the same sitting. (Been there.)

> **Quick reminder**: the **free workbook** available at the book's hub guides you through all of these exercises, in detail. Just go to mindfuldrinkingbook.com to download this excellent, zero-cost resource.

WHAT TO DO: Let's keep this first exercise simple. I'd like you to do **3 things** to assess your recent heavy drinking patterns:

1. As best you can, **reflect on the past 6 months of drinking** and note any instances of **heavy episodic drinking, binging, or extreme binging**. You might consider scrolling through your calendar or checking the Uber history to jog your memory. You're trying to remember when you had **4 drinks or more**. A "drink" is typically about 5 ounces of wine, 12 ounces of regular strength beer, or 1.5 ounces of liquor (the amount in a shot or most mixed drinks).

2. Jot down a few things about each instance of heavy drinking. It's especially important to note the **day, time, place**, and any **co-conspirators**. (**Side note**: The **free workbook** gives you specific places to record this information.)

3. **Make observations** about your heavy drinking episodes over the past 6 months:

   ○ How many are instances of **heavy episodic drinking**?

   ○ How many **binges**? How many **extreme binges**?

   ○ Are there any **patterns** in terms of days, times, or people? Are you binging on weekends with friends, for example? Or maybe at home by yourself, unwinding after work? What's going on around you when this happens?

   ○ On average, how many times did you drink heavily per week and per month?

Don't be hard on yourself if it feels impossible to go back 6 months—most of us can hardly remember what we had for lunch yesterday. Just do your best and make whatever notes you can.

Once you've done this exercise, you'll have a feel for your heavy drinking patterns, which is a healthy step toward understanding your relationship with alcohol.

Remember: Seeing binges before they happen is an ace in the hole for the mindful drinker. If you can do that, you'll be able to cut *them* off before the bartender cuts *you* off.

Chapter 3

Why We Drink, Part I

Creativity and Career Benefits

"They say as soon as you have to cut down on your drinking, you have a drinking problem."

Don Draper

Mad Men did a lot for on-the-clock drinking, exposing us to a world where midday martinis were as common as "paper jam in tray 1." Modern drinkers developed a false nostalgia for an era of wet meetings in smoke-filled rooms, the natural habitat of the 1960s ad exec.

Imbued in the images is an idea: cocktails aren't just props—they symbolize power, virility, and creativity. In other words, drinking (even in excess) is a tool for corporate advancement, upward mobility, and conjuring the greatest car ad of all time.

Don Draper isn't the man in the power suit without his Old-Fashioned. Peggy Olson doesn't climb the ladder until she falls into a whiskey bottle. And without the hooch, the rollicking story of Sterling Cooper would never catch our fancy.

Remarkably, nuggets of *Mad Men* culture have seeped into modern workplaces, as the number embracing alcohol has ballooned. Google, Dropbox, Yelp, and the artist formerly known as Twitter all have company-sponsored drinks on hand.[1] This is surprising given alcohol's connection with workplace problems like sexual harassment. (Or, entirely *un*surprising given the tech sector's boys' club reputation, complete with a history of sexual harassment.[2])

Other than being cooler than the squares at Microsoft, why would so many renowned companies introduce the risks of this "perk"? For the same reason Roger Sterling and Don Draper do: to help workers connect and to grease the wheels of innovation.

In this chapter, we're going to explore the **connection between alcohol and innovation** in the workplace. We'll also learn about the link between alcohol and higher earnings.

It's important to note, however, that you don't have to drink heavily to reap the rewards. In fact, too many servings will hurt more than help. As you read, you might think about how to get these benefits without falling into the trap of overdoing it.

Benefit 1: Creativity and Innovation

The alcohol-creativity connection leans on the concept of "**lateral thinking**," which is a pseudo-scientific term for **creative problem-solving**.[3] When we open a wine bottle without a corkscrew, we're using lateral thinking (and prepping a scathing AirBnb review).

Research has shown a connection between drinking and "aha moments"—sudden breakthroughs of ingenuity. One study had subjects do a "working memory capacity" test, called the Remote Associates Test (RAT).[4] The main task is to tie together three seemingly unrelated words such as "throat," "loser," and "spot" with a fourth word. In this case, the answer is "sore." Sounds easy, but it gets harder.

First, the researchers did a pre-alcohol round of testing to establish a benchmark. Then they gave subjects a carefully measured alcohol dosage based on weight, targeting a BAC between 0.07 and 0.08%—a decent buzz without being drunk.

Compared with non-drinking control groups, intoxicated subjects were quicker and sharper with RAT questions. They also reported solving the questions in aha moments, as answers suddenly came to them. Adding insult to injury, sober groups also reported not having any fun. But the researchers also found the intoxicated subjects performed poorly on "executive function tasks": paying attention, prioritizing, doing what you're supposed to, etc.

It turned out the same neuro-mechanism was behind both testing outcomes, namely a shutdown of the prefrontal cortex (PFC). So we're seeing two simultaneous impacts of drinking: less mental rigidity *and* more creativity. It's worth mentioning that these results have been repeated elsewhere.[5]

There are, of course, limits to what we can learn from drunks solving riddles in a lab. Luckily, there's real world data that supports the alcohol-innovation connection.

The American prohibition era, although an abysmal failure, ended up being a perfect natural experiment for studying the social impacts of alcohol (or the lack thereof). Once alcohol was banned, "wet counties"—where alcohol was legal before prohibition—saw a drop in new patents of up to 18% compared to "dry counties," where alcohol was already illegal.[6]

A few years later, two things happened at the same time: the rise of speakeasies and a rebound in the number of patents. In short, where social drinking was an important part of human connectivity, innovation suffered. It's as if watering holes were petri dishes of American ingenuity, with their fingerprints on one out of every five new ideas.

There was another peculiar observation: In places where patents dropped, the decline was smaller for groups that didn't frequent saloons, including women and certain ethnic groups. This is presumably because they were working under the same sober conditions as always. We may not *need* alcohol to be creative. But if we're used to having it around it helps, giving intoxicated inventors a creative advantage.

The prohibition studies are well-supported by others, especially the academic literature on social capital and collective innovation.[7] Altogether, they indicate that **three benefits** of alcohol often lead to breakthroughs: **social interactions, chance encounters,** and **creative problem-solving.** In sum, alcohol aids innovation by shifting our perspective on problems, while also helping us mold solutions by talking them out.

This is an interesting observation, but one with an important footnote: The creativity benefits don't happen in excess or in isolation. This establishes a **caveat on alcohol's benefits** that consistently resurfaces, namely that they practically disappear when we drink alone.

For perspective, consider a few of the crazy ideas that were originally scribbled out on bar napkins:[8]

- The first digital computer

- The MRI machine

- *Shark Week*

- The ethernet

- Facebook's data center

- Stephen King's *Misery* (and probably any of his books from the 1980s)

- Trickle-down economics (I didn't say they were all were great ideas)

Benefit 2: Career and Money

There are healthy ties between moderate drinking, career prospects, and earnings.

University of Michigan researchers learned that light drinkers had a mean income of $49,000 versus $36,000 for non-drinkers.[9] To see if the relationship was indirect, they took out all the other factors, including education, age, family status, race, and religion. Even then, they still observed a "drinker's bonus" of 10% higher income. Perhaps most importantly, the benefit vanished once the light drinkers crossed into heavy drinking.

An OECD report came to a similar conclusion, noting that "people who are better educated and of higher socioeconomic status are more likely to drink alcohol than others."[10] They also pointed out that while men have traditionally benefited the most from the drinker's bonus, that same connection is now showing up for women, especially in Western society.

We have no way of proving whether drinking actually *causes* these work and wage benefits. But the relationship is powerful. NERDY STATS ALERT: The statistical correlation is so strong that no other intervening variables have been able to weaken it. In simple words, no other explanation makes a stronger statistical case.

So where does this relationship come from? Most likely from one (or more) of four sources:

1. Drinking leads to **more effective networking**, which in turn leads to better connections and improved career prospects.

2. Good networkers and high achievers are **extroverts** who are more likely to drink in the first place. The egg comes before the chicken.

3. Drinking makes you a **more creative and productive worker**. This gives drinkers the upper hand in climbing the ranks.

4. Drinking is connected to **elevated status** (i.e. being "cool"), while non-drinking is associated with the lack thereof or possibly lower status.

The first three explanations have obvious mechanisms lying underneath. Drinking helps colleagues become better connected, which is the basic definition of networking. It's especially helpful for those of us who feel awkward in networking situations. If that doesn't get the job done, the assist to productivity and creativity will help us wow the suits in upper management.

The fourth explanation is closely connected to the other 3, but is a bit sadder. In essence, it suggests that social status gets us into the right crowd—that drinking is cool and not drinking is lame. It's hard to accept that intelligent adults could get caught up in such perceptions. But a **workplace connection between drinking and street cred** is exactly what we find.

A Canadian study showed that binge drinking led to higher social status and career advancement for men.[11] The authors even titled the article "Drinking to Reach the Top," a twist on the idea of sleeping your way to the top. Ready for the punchline? They concluded that binging for male coworkers is an indication of power and masculinity. The catch, however, was that if they ever got sick, their status eroded. In other words, tying one on made you cool until you couldn't handle your shit. The mob is fickle.

These same results are repeated elsewhere.[12] College students who drink are better integrated into campus communities, have higher social status, and commonly hold organizational leadership positions.[13] Binge drinking in Chinese work culture has also been tied to trust networks and status.[14] Two conclusions emerge; First, alcohol impacts social status; Second, there is pressure to engage in this behavior to avoid the abyss of social isolation.

Evidence from ancient Sumer to the Bolivian Amazon tells a similar story: Strangers were often greeted with a drink, and declining the offer could have deadly consequences. Why? Because alcohol is critical to building trust between strangers, some of whom are potential enemies. And the ability to hold one's alcohol was a sign of reliability and virtue.[15]

On the flip side, non-drinkers were often viewed with suspicion, which put them at a disadvantage when it came to creating alliances and trust networks. The term "water drinker" was used as an insult in ancient Greece. You had to drink to show you were trustworthy.

I'm convinced, with zero evidence, that this is also why getting smashed at toga parties became a thing. What was once true in Greece is now true in Greek life and, believe it or not, the workplace. But now instead of "deadly consequences," turning down a drink just relegates you to a lower social status.

I like to think that we're better than this now, that we understand abstainers have good reasons for their choices. Still, many of us leer at the non-drinker, wondering what their problem is. Apparently, we're the latest in a long history of judgmental assholes and drug pushers who insist that others drink to prove they're one of us. And if they need their hair held back for them, they're weaklings.

Things shouldn't be this way. But, as Tupac would say, I was given this world, I didn't make it.

Thanks to Gen Z's sober tendencies, getting tanked might soon get you shunned rather than promoted. For now, though, the historical trends are still in effect. When we drink with coworkers, we get a leg up on promotions, better working conditions, increased social capital, and maybe even access to different careers. And *a lot* of that stems from the status we acquire from being one of the cool kids.

In any case, it's clear that the bulk of these benefits stems from an association between alcohol and relationship building. There were so many angles to this that I had to add a second chapter on the benefits of alcohol, with an exclusive focus on social connections, friendship, and love. All of it shows why humans have kept alcohol around for so long, and why we're not poised to ditch it any time soon.

Chapter Summary

- Alcohol improves **"lateral thinking"** (creative problem-solving) and worsens our performance on **"executive function tasks"** (doing what you're supposed to).

- Both effects are caused by a shut-down of the **pre-frontal cortex**, the part of our brain that regulates **executive functions** (e.g. decision-making, planning, and moderating behavior.)

- Alcohol provides **3 benefits** that impact **human ingenuity**: social interactions, chance encounters, and creative problem-solving.

- Light and moderate drinking is associated with **higher earnings** and **enhanced career prospects**.

- This is most likely due to more effective networking, extroversion, creativity and productivity, or elevated social status.

- These social benefits evaporate when we drink alone or in excess.

Chapter 4

Why We Drink, Part 2

Friends, Relationships, and Romance

"Champagne for my real friends and real pain for my sham friends."

Tom Waits

I n April 2020, at the height of the Covid-19 shutdowns, a Gallup survey found that 1 in 4 U.S. adults reported feeling lonely much of the previous day.[1] These staggering rates of social detachment were surely impacted by the pandemic. And yet, they hadn't changed much by October 2022, when the same survey found 1 in 5 still felt isolated.

This was no longer just a relic of the pandemic, but an extension of modern culture and technology, which continued to erode the quality of our social connections. This problem isn't uniquely American. In fact, it mirrors other Western societies, including the EU, where social isolation doubled during the pandemic and continues to be problematic.

The generational gaps in loneliness are equally alarming, but surprising. Gallup's 2023 poll found **24% of young people** (18-29) reported loneliness versus **13% of those 65 and older**.

This data falls in line with other surveys. A similar one by Cigna asked respondents if they felt lonely on a "pretty regular basis", which is a more liberal measure of loneliness.[2] When posed this way, they found that roughly **half of baby boomers** expressed anxieties of social detachment versus **70% of millennials** and **80% of Gen Z** respondents. This is an unexpected twist on the link between age and social isolation,[3] which typically suggests that older people are lonelier than those prancing around in their youth.

It's clear that social isolation is a problem that's poised to worsen with time. More importantly, this problem comes with heavy individual costs: mental acuity, physical mobility, even showering daily. All these negative outcomes are linked to a lack of social connectivity.

Former Surgeon General Vivek Murthy wrote that "loneliness...(is) associated with a reduction in lifespan similar to that caused by smoking 15 cigarettes a day and even greater than that associated with obesity."[4] If that's true, it means anyone battling solitude would oddly benefit from a "14-a-day" smokers' club, a stark sign of the risks of loneliness.

You might be expecting me to say that drinking equals friends and is therefore a panacea for loneliness. I wish it were so simple. Alcohol's ability to bring people together is well-documented, but it's no simple fix for anything that ails society or the individual. It's more accurate to say that drinking opens friendship opportunities that *can* lead to better social connectivity.

We should also remember that alcohol abuse destroys relationships—drink too much, and we're more likely to end up talking to a wall than an ear. That said, research shows that moderate drinking is connected to a healthy social life. This is likely because of the facilitating role that alcohol plays in social situations.

Alcohol and Bonding, Explained

The neurological effects of alcohol play a direct role in social bonding. This phenomenon starts with **endorphins**, which tether themselves to opiate receptors in the brain.[5] Studies have shown that endorphins are **central to social bonding**—we become happier, less stressed, and more affable. We also get a boost in self-confidence, which explains delusions that we're more attractive and better dancers. The result is a greater willingness to connect, commiserate, and commingle.

University of Pittsburgh researchers randomly assigned strangers into groups of three. Half of the groups were given alcohol; the others were given a non-alcoholic placebo. Then the researchers analyzed each group's social interactions to see how the drinkers differed from the control group.

Facial and speech analysis revealed that alcohol led to more "true" smiles and "expressive reciprocity" (people genuinely smiling back). In fact, alcohol facilitated so-called "golden moments," which was when all group members smiled simultaneously.

Self-reports backed up these observations. Alcohol-infused groups reported higher social bonding and conversational connectedness.[6] Hard to tell from the statistical analysis, but it sounds like one group was on the verge of a 3-way make out session. (Or maybe I was just lonely when I read it.)

Drinkers have long sensed that this effect exists outside of experiments. We're full of anecdotes about instant alcohol friends—people we drank with but otherwise wouldn't have noticed. This is often how work relationships push across professional boundaries and into something closer resembling friendship.

We've long assumed it was the alcohol. But we no longer have to assume—there's ample evidence that the social benefits of moderate drinking are real.

The Social Payouts of Alcohol

The main social benefit of alcohol is **expanded social networks**.

When French public health officials carried out a study of 150,000 people, they discovered that moderate drinkers fared better on a series of health indicators than both non-drinkers and heavy drinkers.[7] One benefit was something called "optimal social status," an indicator measured by surveying participants about their social lives. On this measure, moderate drinkers ranked highest. Teetotalers came in dead last.

The same study revealed that nondrinkers were the most likely to live alone. This single fact could explain a big part of the abstention-loneliness connection, given that those living alone are more likely to report feeling disconnected. More importantly, non-drinkers generally didn't *feel* as good as other participants, even heavy drinkers. Something about abstention produced malaise.

To be fair, the causal flow could run in the opposite direction—malaise causes abstention, also known as the "sick quitter" phenomenon. In any case, you'd think non-drinkers would reap the health benefits and feel better than the rest of us. Yet this simply isn't the case. For whatever reason, while abstaining from alcohol has obvious health benefits, **there are invisible costs that *can* outweigh them.**

One thing that isn't lonely is the French study. Another study from Denmark came to a strikingly similar conclusion: Drinkers, on average, benefited from higher social status. A survey of 250,000 American adults found the same connection.[8] And a 50,000-participant study out of England delivered resounding conclusions that non-drinkers and heavy drinkers suffered from a lack of social support far more often than moderate[9] drinkers did.

(Quick side note: The American study also found that non-drinkers were far more likely to never marry, confirming my long-held suspicion that sober dating is torture.)

These findings add up to what Robin Dunbar called "the functional benefits of (modest) alcohol consumption."[10] Dunbar and his team observed people in live bar settings, then had them fill out questionnaires. The team hoped to learn about alcohol's impact on social networks, conversation, support systems, and social trust. They found out that "social drinkers have more friends on whom they can depend" and "feel more engaged with...their local community."

In a plot-thickening twist, Dunbar found that this relationship was heavily conditioned by the setting. People who frequent small, neighborhood pubs are better integrated with their community and have more close friendships than those who frequent bigger bars.

This relationship probably exists because drinkers in smaller pubs congregated in smaller groups. This led to more intimate conversations and, by extension, deeper connections. Simply put, alcohol helps us socialize, but environment matters.

It's important to point out that you don't *need* alcohol to be socially connected—it's just a tendency. Non-drinkers have vibrant support systems all the time. But the alcohol-friendship connection is both real and powerful.

With the exception of our mothers at birth, every person we've ever met is a stranger. Alcohol helps us trust those new faces and opens the door to a closer connection. From there, it's just a numbers game: more social encounters + fewer social inhibitions = healthier social networks. We just have to keep in mind that our drinking has to be social and moderate to reap these benefits.

Every once in a while, one of the strangers we meet is cute. If they think we are too, there's potential for a new bonding ritual: dating.

The "Demographic Time Bomb"

In 2015, Japanese prime minister Shinzo Abe was scrambling to find solutions for a growing problem: the previous 20 years had seen a crash in marriage and birth rates, resulting in a population decline of 1 million people since 2010.[11]

Economists, aware of Japan's aging population, abandoned their calm demeanors to declare that a "demographic time bomb" was on the horizon. The problem, in short, was that many young Japanese weren't enticed by dating.[12] They found the entire courtship process to be awkward, so they were opting out en masse.

Abe's government immediately threw money at the problem. A lot of it. Tokyo allocated $24 million to the cause of *konkatsu* ("marriage hunting"), hoping it would promote a rise in birth rates. This funding led to publicly funded matchmaking services whose sole enterprise was to awkwardly push young singles together until they made babies.[13]

How does a desperate government move the dating needle? By hosting *machikon*, alcohol-infused mixers where daters could play footsie, pair up, and make some bad choices.[14] This is the government equivalent of a late-night text begging for sex. (Ask not what your country can do for you, ask what hasty decision you can make for your country. And preferably tonight.)

By 2020, 1 in 6 Japanese fiancés had met their spouse through konkatsu services.[15] This was a drastic increase from about 1 in 20 in 2015, when Abe's government started throwing money at the baby problem. That's a 220% increase in 5 short years. And if a young dater had any konkatsu experience at all, there was a 50/50 chance they ended up marrying a match they met through those services.

The results were clear: konkatsu and machikon worked. It turns out, to nobody's surprise, that baiting people into relationships is much easier when you soak the room with sake and Sapporo. All the better if it's donated by the unwitting taxpayer.

The Japanese government leaned on a social reality backed by research: Alcohol has been shown to help daters get to the finish line, facilitating the dating connections that lead to relationships and, eventually, marriage.

Alcohol and Dating

In a galaxy far, far away, boys married the fetching girl next door. So long as the letterman jacket was snug, it was on.

Most of us are glad times have changed. But today's dating world is a mixed bag of its own. Modern dating culture is app-driven, mostly blind, and full of lies. In my dating app days—okay, years—three filters were automatic: religion, education, and drinker status. I wanted my Tinderellas secular, smart, and social. Still, even with all the curating, half the time I'd be shocked at who I met.

My case, like many, shows why modern dating is a dive into a deep unknown. It's also why today's dating rituals breed extra anxiety. What if they're an awkward freak? What if they have eyes and realize I'm "a few extra pounds" and not "athletic"? What if they're—gulp—a Republican?! (They're jokes, stay calm.)

To deal with it all, we make our dates quick and wet. Drinking and dating is so widespread that 86% of daters report drinking during a first date.[16] And about half of those tipped the bottle *before* a date.

> **Fun Fact:** According to Alcohol.org, if a date gets to 5 alcoholic drinks, there's a 51% chance it leads to sex. **Quick math:** That means 5 drinks on back-to-back dates equals a 98% chance of chlamydia. Hope you got this message on time.

So what is it about alcohol that helps dates? In a nutshell, it helps us bond. Wet dates had more elation, happiness, and open expression, which are the building blocks of intimacy.[17] Our confidence spikes, we laugh easier, and we like each other more. The upshot is that moderate drinking helps us date successfully, which makes it more likely that we'll get married.

A (totally scientific) Plenty of Fish survey found that casual drink dates were one of three types likely to lead to marriage.[18] The other two were grabbing a meal and taking a walk. **Conclusion:** Think hard before drinking on a walking food tour date—it's basically an engagement.

Alcohol and Marriage

In 1987, a California research team learned that moderate drinkers were half as likely to be *un*married as teetotalers. For whatever reason, they simply made their way to the altar more frequently.

This finding got repeated over and over until it became clear that non-drinkers suffered from some kind of dating disadvantage. Maybe it's that sober dating is grueling. Or that the dating pool shallows when you refuse to have a drink. Whatever the case, the connection is there and it's significant.

The path goes something like this: Outside of mail-order brides and reality TV, marriage is an outcome of dating. If we feel good about a date, we get a second date. Then a third. This goes on until someone leaves enough underwear in the other's hamper to change their address. Eventually, the more naïve partner thinks there's enough money for a wedding and proposes marriage. The couple goes on to spend a small fortune and constantly fights about venues, DJs, bands, chicken, beef, and who's invited. (I know I'm not alone.)

Once again, we can credit alcohol's drug properties for the straightening of Cupid's arrow. Once in the body, alcohol bears a striking resemblance to oxytocin,[19] commonly referred to as "the love horm one."[20] Both substances make us more trusting, more empathetic, and less anxious. They also heighten our sense of intimacy and, in turn, our reactions to romantic partners.[21] Sprinkle in better chances of mutual attraction and sexual intercourse, and it's clear why alcohol turns our swipes into likes.

Interestingly, alcohol also influences our perceptions of potential mates. Drinkers are attracted to fellow drinkers. If someone is a non-drinker, we easily interpret this as a lack of compatibility. (I guess the phrase "It's not you, it's me" actually means "It's not you, it's your glass of water.")

Keep in mind that roughly 70% of people in their prime dating years (ages 21 to 35) drink alcohol. If you're sober, the dating pool suddenly becomes a bathtub. While this doesn't doom non-drinking daters to failure, it does shift the odds and partly explains the connection to successful dating and marriage.

Alcohol and Marriage Quality

The reward for stumbling your way to nuptials is a marriage to maintain. (50% success rate, I'm sure you'll be fine.) More good news: alcohol can help here, too.

Research on marital quality has shown that newlyweds who drink together rated their marriages more positively than those who drank separately *and* those who didn't drink at all.[22]

Similarly, retired couples who drank together reported fewer negative issues in their marriages.[23] (**Author's note:** It's interesting that newlyweds describe how "good" things are, while older couples describe how "not bad" they are. Something to look forward to.)

In long-married couples, moderate drinking often led to sexual intimacy and, consequently,[24] more frequent sex than non-drinking couples. This jibes with the dating research showing a connection between alcohol and the chances of sex on a date.

Finally, and for the first time, I'm happy to report my own (totally scientific) home research on alcohol, sex, and marriage. There are two key findings to report; 1) roughly 25% of the time it produces spikes in freakiness; 2) get permission first, or you'll be getting freaky all by your lonesome. (Quick acknowledgment: I'd like to thank my employer, Dallas College, for unwittingly funding this study.)

Here's why moderate drinking helps marriages: it influences a couple's social lives, shared interests, and what's called "complementarity"—similarity between couples. Partners who drink moderately find more in common and share more activities. Simply put, they enjoy each other more and in different ways. All these relationship traits are associated with marriage longevity and quality.[25]

The effect on sex is an extension of the drug effects, especially euphoria. It's important, however, to understand that the benefits evaporate when only one partner drinks. This is called "incongruency." And if that partner's solo drinking is heavy, it commonly leads to marital strife and divorce.[26] Finally, anything past moderate drinking erases the sex benefits, as it inhibits both sexual arousal and performance.[27]

What About the Health Benefits?

Dazed and Confused, probably the finest cinematic achievement of the 90s, squeezed a lot of messages into an hour and a half. Tucked into the edges of teenage rebellion, hazing rituals, and underage drinking were more subtle jabs at the culture of the times. For starters, the movie's most repeated line—"alright, alright, alright"—was uttered by a lovable character who, by today's standards, is an abhorrent sexual predator. Times change, I guess.

In the convenience store scene, 14-year-old Mitch walks up to buy a "sixer" for the senior boys. The scene stuck with me because it resonated—I was a 16-year-old boy carrying a fake ID in my wallet. But it also took a jab at 1970s ignorance that I never forgot.

Just as Mitch confidently walks up to buy beer, the clerk gives advice to a pregnant mother. "Remember to eat a green thing every day and have lots of calcium. It's very important for young mothers to have *lots* of calcium." The clerk then hands her a pack of cigarettes just as she takes a drag from the one in her hand and says, "See you tomorrow."

Even in the 90s, we knew to laugh. What made it funny wasn't just that she was smoking. It was that swaths of Americans in the 1970s hadn't yet learned how detrimental it is to your health. And this was despite the medical science linking smoking to cancer as early as the 1950s.[28]

To their discredit, Big Tobacco somehow managed to deflect the truth for six decades, until finally admitting in 2006 that smoking was a known carcinogen.[29] How did they cloud the truth about smoking for so long? With strategic, focused misinformation. Sure, we got the message eventually. But it took time. As Matthew McConaughey's David Wooderson might say, "That's what I like about these untruths, man—I get older, so do they."

Philip Morris isn't alone. Exxon knew about climate change in the 1970s. Facebook swears social media isn't addictive. And Disney denies sneaking dicks into kids' movies. Big Alcohol pushes a similar, equally false narrative about the health benefits found in bottles. In fact, they've been as intentional and mendacious as the others.

One medical research team noted that 24 out of 26 "alcohol industry organizations" distorted or misrepresented evidence of health risks.[30] This means they are massaging data or spotlighting convenient, unproven conclusions.

Such practices have the effect of muddying the water on medical research so that drinkers will feel either confused or emboldened—or both. Big Alcohol's propaganda has also been successful. Here are some **prevailing misconceptions** about alcohol and health:

- There's no clear link between **alcohol and cancer**. (There is.)

- Moderate drinking is **risk-free**. (It isn't.)

- Drinking **improves sleep** quality. (Not a chance.)

- Alcohol **reduces anxiety**. (Quite the opposite.)

- Alcohol **improves sexual performance**. (This one's only true for me.)

- Alcohol **risks can be neutralized** by good dietary habits, hydration, or supplements. (Don't even get me started on the supplements industry.)

- Increased tolerance is a sign that your body is handling alcohol well. (That's one way of looking at it.)

- Certain types of alcohol—especially red wine—are good for
  you.

Each of these statements is pure fiction. Yet, we hear them stated and
restated constantly in media and (shockingly) even medical circles. Why
might this be the case? Because nothing makes better clickbait than
studies on the purported benefits of alcohol. One Italian study on wine
and sex will produce fifty blog posts titled "Bizarre Facts About Wine
and Your Sex Drive."[31]

This rush to inform is connected to another reality: drinkers *really*
want the health benefits to be true. It's the same confirmation bias we
see in politics. We happily accept what we hope is true while summarily
rejecting what's inconvenient. The article on drinking and mind-blow-
ing sex is cutting-edge journalism; the one on drinking and cancer is
alarmist drivel. Share the first, shun the second.

Complicating matters is that legitimate research does show limited
health benefits from alcohol. The claim about red wine being healthy
is an ideal example. This perception grew from a 1992 *Lancet* study
on the so-called "French paradox," which saw people having low heart
disease rates despite eating high amounts of saturated fat.[32] Subsequent
studies often confirmed that alcohol can reduce some risks, especially
for cardiovascular mortality and heart disease.[33]

But these studies rarely emphasize that the benefits rely on moderate
consumption (1 to 2 daily drinks with no binges). They also don't consider the risks that are added in other areas—hypertension, cancer, etc.
Most importantly, these studies ignore all the other ways that alcohol
damages physical health, especially when we zoom past moderation.

Here's the **simple truth about alcohol's physical benefits**: when
balanced against the risks, **there are none**. This inconvenient truth
was affirmed by another *Lancet* study, this time from 2018, which em-
phatically announced that "no level of alcohol consumption improves
health."[34]

The alcohol industry has quickly done damage control, and the heart
stuff is their best argument.[35] But concluding that alcohol is therefore
healthy is like embracing smoking because it prevents Parkinson's d
isease.[36] Drinkers, like smokers in the 70s, would do well to accept
independent medical science.

In the end, I'm confident that untruths about alcohol's health benefits will join the relics of days past, ending up on the same shelf as pregnant smokers and doctors touting cigarettes. We might even get a good one-liner out of it when *Dazed and Confused II* finally comes out.

This conversation about health liabilities is a good prelude to the next chapter, which discusses those risks in detail. Fair warning: It's the least uplifting part of the book. But this evil is as necessary as any other.

Chapter Summary

- Alcohol's role in **social bonding** is rooted in **endorphins**, which play a central role in establishing social connections.

- This produces the **social benefits** of alcohol, which include expanded social networks, higher social status, and greater social support.

- Alcohol helps **dating** by increasing open expression and enhancing intimacy. This may be why moderate drinkers are half as likely to be unmarried than non-drinkers.

- Alcohol also impacts **marriage quality**, with moderate drinking couples reporting higher satisfaction than non-drinking couples.

- Moderate drinking in marriage is also linked with more frequent sex, shared interests, and "complementarity."

- While these social benefits are real, the **health benefits** of drinking are a myth. When balanced against the health risks, they simply don't exist.

Chapter 5

Why We Should Cut Back

The Risks of Alcohol

"Clear alcohols are for rich women on diets."

Ron Swanson

The buildup to my 40th birthday was overshadowed by the third trimester of our second pregnancy. April, our youngest daughter, arrived two days after I celebrated the milestone, smashing together two contrasting experiences—birth and advancing age. I was ecstatic, but once again felt the weight of parenthood on my shoulders.

In and of itself, turning 40 makes you think twice about age and longevity. Coupling it with another child gave those thoughts sharper teeth. April would be ten during my second colonoscopy and 20 when I started drinking Ensure for breakfast. As you might imagine, I became acutely sensitive to the distance I'd have to run to keep pace.

In response to our looming age and parenting crisis, my wife Susie suggested we turn to Audible. Our first stop was Sara Gottfried's *Younger,* a manual for aging gracefully. We were immediately filled with regrets, as the intro chapter more quickly inspired suicidal thoughts than good health.

Get this: Cellular decline ramps up at 40, which is also the start of "middle age." (Perfect timing.) In case that wasn't jarring enough, Gottfried also mentions that senescence—the sad ending of cellular growth—is already happening. Suddenly, death felt closer. Maybe better, too. My sullen partner turned to me and said, "Can we stop? This is depressing."

Unlike Gottfried, I've put the sad parts in my book off until Chapter 5. (You're welcome.) But sadly, it's time to browse the latest research on alcohol's health risks. While it won't brighten up a weekend, knowing the risks comes with a **major benefit**: we're more likely to **nix bad habits when we know their real costs**.

Understanding risk is critical for motivating change. On the flip side, *not* hearing the truth might keep you happy today, but you'll be unarmed by ignorance in the long haul.

That said, if you find this is overwhelming or unhelpful, feel free to move on to the next chapter. Most importantly, please—pretty please—don't panic. What I discuss in this chapter are risks, not inevitable outcomes. As such, they're hardly worth emotional spirals or late-night WebMD searches.

(**Author's note:** What's here carries risks for the messenger, too. Unless you hate being invited to parties, *don't* bring up alcohol risks at one.)

Risk 1: Bad Choices

Alcohol's most immediate risk is stupidity. Each serving nudges us closer to a loss of self-control, bad decision-making, and poor dating choices. (Don't worry, I'm sure they'll call.)

Taken to extremes, these risks multiply like gremlins. Experienced drinkers are acutely aware of how foolhardy they can be after multiple servings. And these mistakes can quickly go from embarrassing to deadly. Consider, for example, how alcohol impacts accidents:

- A blood alcohol concentration (BAC) of 0.05% (a drink or two) increases the chances of a **car accident** by 100% (x2). When BAC gets to 0.08%—the legal driving limit in most states—the **odds triple**. By the time you get to 0.10%, they've **quintupled**.[1]

- Alcohol accounts for up to **18% of ER visits**, a majority of which are serious head injuries.[2]

- An estimated 1,825 college students from 18 to 24 years old **die each year** due to alcohol-related injuries.

- Roughly **one-third of fatal and nonfatal falls** involve alcohol. And you're **60 times more likely** to fall when your BAC reaches 0.08%.

- Alcohol is implicated in over **3 million incidents of criminal violence** each year. It's more likely to be a factor when the attacker and victim know each other.

- An estimated 68% of drowning deaths involve alcohol.

I should mention that you don't have to be inebriated for these injury odds to kick in—it only takes pedestrian BACs that most of us reach in an average drinking session. Apparently, it doesn't take much for the risks of stupidity to kick in.

Risk 2: Cancer

Unfortunately, alcohol is officially on the carcinogen list. Two Red Bull and Vodkas might make you *feel* immortal. But each one gently pushes the cancer meter into the red.

The leading hypothesis for the alcohol-cancer connection is the **toxic nature of acetaldehyde,** the main byproduct of metabolizing alcohol. In heavy drinkers, acetaldehyde builds up exponentially, spreading its toxicity to cells. And when free radicals attach themselves to DNA, it makes the genetic mutations that cause cancer more likely.

Medical science has gained clarity on alcohol's links to specific cancers. In fact, the National Toxicology Program connects it to at least **five types**: oral, esophageal, liver, colorectal, and breast.[3] Here's a rundown of the key statistics by type:

- Oral cancer

  - The average person runs a 1% chance of oral cancer, which affects the mouth and throat. Moderate drinking bumps this up to a **3% likelihood**, while heavy drinking *quintuples* the odds to about a **5% chance.**

- The odds are even higher for men who drink heavily. And they skyrocket after men hit 50, effectively sharpening alcohol's blade with age.

- Esophageal cancer

  - Heavy drinkers are almost **5 times more likely** to acquire esophageal squamous cell carcinoma, which is the most common esophageal cancer.[4] Moderate drinkers are **2.25 times more likely**.[5]

  - Esophageal cancer is deadly, having a **five-year survival rate of only 20%** (1 in 5).[6] Given it's fatality, any increase in risk is significant.

- Liver cancer

  - The National Cancer Institute reports a 1% lifetime chance of liver cancer on average. Moderate drinking only **increases the odds to a 1.1% chance**. But heavy drinking doubles the odds to **2%**.[7]

  - Liver cancer has a **five-year survival rate of about 20% (1 in 5)**, meaning it's in a dead heat with esophageal cancer when it comes to mortality.

- Colorectal cancer

  - The average person has a 4% chance (1 in 25) of colon cancer in their lifetime, making it the **2nd most common type** on our list.

  - Moderate drinking increases the odds to a **5% chance**, while heavy drinking takes it to a **6% chance**.[8]

  - Alcohol also impacts colon cancer **survival rates**, which sit at 37% for drinkers and 76% for non-drinkers. That's **half the chance of survival**. This is because alcohol-related cases tend to be discovered at more advanced stages, meaning more metastases and shorter lifespans.[9]

At this point, you might be feeling overwhelmed by cancer statistics. Again, it's not my intention to burden you with this information, but to arm you. I want you to understand alcohol's true weight, especially when it comes to heavy drinking.

The previous list had 4 cancers, which means there's one more to discuss. (Just one more, I promise.) The last one is especially important, which is why I broke it off into its own section.

Risk 3: Breast Cancer

About 12% of women in the U.S. (1 in 8) will develop breast cancer in their lifetime.[10] That's roughly 280,000 new cases[11] per year, just in America. It is by far the most prevalent of the five types of cancer discussed here. Any risk increase from alcohol is therefore significant to public health and dangerous to the individual.

Alcohol-related breast cancer isn't just linked to acetaldehyde, free radicals, and oxidative stress. Those three play their role. But a more direct line is drawn to hormones, including heightened levels of progesterone or estrogen, which are indicated in 2 out of 3 cases.[12] Cancerous cells are often found to be ER-positive, meaning they have receptors that attach to estrogen hormones.[13]

As drinkers' fates would have it, alcohol causes spikes in estrogen. This is likely due to the presence of **phytoestrogens**—estrogen-like substances from plants—in alcoholic beverages.[14] Consequently, even at moderate levels, drinking brings hormonal fluctuations. (Side note: This may also explain why alcoholic cirrhosis in men is often comorbid with testicular failure.)

The most striking statistics describe the risks **per alcohol serving**, defined in one study as a **7-10% increase per daily drink**.[15] By this measure, a woman consuming **three daily drinks** moves the original 12% chance **as high as 16%**. Another study noted that **heavy drinking** balloons the risk to **as high as 19%** (almost 1 in 5).[16]

The truth is that no level is safe. Even light consumption (one daily drink) nudges the meter to 13.2%—a small change by comparison, but significant. In fact, one study darkly noted that almost 1 in 5 alcohol-related diagnoses are attributable to just *one* daily drink.[17]

Put into perspective, these numbers deliver a somber reality:

In terms of human suffering and societal costs, breast cancer has the ignominious distinction of being the **most impacted by alcohol**. One study noted that 10% of new cases are alcohol-related. This translated to 28,000 yearly cases by way of drinking[18] That's just in the U.S.

There is, however, a sliver of good news: the five-year survival rate for breast cancer is about 90%.[19] Patients will suffer, but at least their odds of survival are decent.

Risk 4: Heart Disease

Excessive drinking is closely connected to higher risks of stroke, high blood pressure, heart failure, and cardiomyopathy.

There's an ongoing tug-of-war on alcohol and heart health. Studies have repeatedly made the connection between moderate alcohol intake and a lower risk of heart disease. This has especially been touted by the wine industry as a benefit of red wine, which is associated with higher levels of good (HDL) cholesterol.[20] Another possible source is the antioxidant properties of certain drinks, another claim that's happily parroted by vintners.

Cardiovascular benefits are the best support for the "a little bit is good for you" arguments. But I'm suspicious of anyone—or any entity—who tries to suggest that alcohol has health benefits. We really want it to be true. But as I mentioned in Chapter 4, it's just self-supporting nonsense backed by cherry-picked statistics.

I'll raise **three issues** on the cardio benefits:

1. The cardio relationship is **not cut-and-dry**. The red wine benefit, for example, may be rooted in socioeconomics—Zinfandel drinkers have good health benefits and shop at Whole Foods. Many studies fail to isolate alcohol from other factors, making their conclusions dubious.

2. Even if there are grains of truth to these arguments, heart benefits only exist for people **without heart-related conditions**. So if you have cardiomyopathy, high blood pressure, irregular heart rhythm, stroke history, or high triglycerides, the "benefit" part is misleading. Alcohol won't help these conditions. To be fair, moderate drinking doesn't seem to worsen them, either.[21]

3. Any heart benefits are likely **canceled out** by other risks. These include inflammation, oxidative stress, cellular decline, and circulatory changes due to alcohol.[22]

Even if we assume there's truth in the heart benefits of alcohol, it's important to remember the other risks that come with any amount of drinking. It's a trade-off. If we stay moderate, it's fair to say that our heart is the least of our concerns. But don't fool yourself—drinking to be heart-healthy is mostly a convenient story. Real heart benefits still run through the traditional avenues of exercise and a healthy diet. (You hate me, right?)

Risk 5: Poor Sleep

A typical night's sleep (seven to eight hours) includes six or seven REM cycles. With alcohol in your system, you only get two or three. This happens, ironically, because you sleep deeply for the first few hours, so deeply that you don't rise into REM sleep. Once you're past your alcohol-induced deep sleep, the rest of your sleep is shallow and scattered.[23]

> There's something we need to get through our bed heads: Alcohol, especially in high quantities, **cuts our REM sleep in half**. This is why multiple servings are so disruptive to our natural sleeping patterns and often cause morning fog.

These negative sleep effects are caused by the release of stimulants, which your body uses to counteract alcohol's depressive effects. The result, as you're groggily aware, is that you wake up at weird hours and feel uneasy. This is especially true after a binge. By morning, you feel listless and struggle to face a new day.

As the sleepless nights pile on, they have increasingly detrimental effects on our health. Consider the following negative outcomes of poor sleep:

- Your body **can't fully regenerate** overnight. This affects your immune system and thus your ability to fight infections.

- You're **more likely to overeat** and **less likely to exercise** the following day.

- You reach for other **stimulants**, such as coffee, contributing to the up-down cycle you're already struggling with.

- You become **short-tempered**, allowing little things to irk you more than they should. If your spouse drinks, you've probably been on the receiving end of this injustice. (Yeah, I went there.)

For these reasons, poor sleep has become connected with serious health problems, including obesity, diabetes, heart disease, and cancer. If you want to count more sheep than copays, it behooves you to avoid extra alcohol servings, especially just before bed.

Risk 6: Stress, Anxiety, and Depression

Alcohol is a common means of coping with stress, anxiety, and depression. Ironically, it also **exacerbates all these conditions**. Men are more prominent stress drinkers, but women with higher stress levels also report higher alcohol intake.[24]

At the same time, people who drink heavily have higher amounts of **cortisol** circulating in their body, making them more prone to extreme stress and anxiety. Alcohol's disruptions to sleep also come into play—our bodies rely on restorative sleep to deal with daily stressors. When we don't sleep well, our ability to manage stress is compromised. This cycle, in which drinking begets what it's meant to relieve, is a vicious one.

Heavy drinking is also connected to **chronic depression**. In fact, almost **one-third** of people with major depression also struggle with alc ohol.[25] Some argue that depression could be causing excessive drinking rather than the reverse. But there's no need to argue over chickens and eggs—it's likely a two-way street.

Keep in mind that alcohol is a depressant. Any amount brings our body down, and copious amounts do so even more. As such, drinking does nothing to help symptoms of depression. In fact, it makes antidepressants less effective.

Risk 7: Weight Gain

Weight gain is a big reason why people cut back on drinking. We deny it for a while, but eventually alcohol's role in our expanding waistline is hard to ignore. By 40, we're wrestling with the fact that "fit" and "tipsy" are competing values. It's not just about beer bellies—all kinds of alcohol can have this effect.

Alcohol causes weight gain (or sabotages weight loss) for 5 main reasons:

1. **It stops you from burning fat.** This is because your body focuses on processing alcohol, which shuts down your metabolism.[26] Also, when the liver is processing alcohol—a toxin—it breaks down fats less efficiently.[27]

2. **It's high in calories.** Most alcoholic beverages have between 110 and 150 calories per serving.[28] Every single one is an "empty" calorie without nutritional value.

3. **It causes overeating.** There's a strong connection between alcohol and poor diet, including increased hunger, less satiation, and cravings for unhealthy foods. With time, the late night Taco Bell runs take a toll.[29] (Decisions, decisions, decisions.)

4. **It causes hormone imbalances.** Alcohol can wreak havoc on thyroid function, among other glands. This leads to increased cortisol levels, which in turn has been linked to weight gain.

5. **It interferes with sleep.** Sleep is critical for maintaining a healthy weight,[30] and as previously mentioned, alcohol keeps us from getting high-quality sleep.

Get excited because there's two pieces of good news. (Three for women.)

First, moderate drinking is ***not* associated with weight gain**.[31] Second, some evidence suggests moderate drinking has a ***protective* effect** on weight gain—if we keep the servings down, our pants size should follow. Finally, a bonus for the ladies: men who drink are more prone to weight gain than women who drink. (Take that, Y chromosome.)

More good news: the alcohol industry—always keen on keeping us drunk and happy—has rushed to offer a host of **low-calorie** and **low-carb options**. Hence the surge in ultra-light beers, low-calorie wines, hard seltzers, and skinny margaritas, to name a few. Luckily, drinks like these typically have the added benefit of a lower alcohol by volume (ABV), so we can cut calories and servings at the same time.

I've fully embraced low-calorie/low-ABV options and have found they're a godsend for cutting servings. Sure, you can often taste the difference compared to OG versions. But in the long run, the low-calorie juice is probably worth the squeeze.

Risk 8: Feeling Shitty

It's good to arm ourselves with knowledge about *all* the risks. But there's one I haven't talked about, and it's probably high on your list of motivators: feeling like ass.

All the things I've discussed so far clearly play into this. You don't immediately think alcohol is making you anxious, disrupting your sleep, or spiking your cancer odds. You just know your experience of it—headaches, nausea, the shakes, all that.

The more this happens (and as it worsens with age), the more problematic drinking becomes. Childless people can often sleep in, giving them a bit more rope. Parents get no such relief. For us, sleeping in was replaced long ago by kids demanding waffles with "chechup." (I pick my battles.)

In the utopia of youth, hangovers ended at about noon. Today, they span multiple days. Rat studies indicate the **age-hangover connection** is due to a **diminishing capacity to detoxify acetaldehyde**.[32] It's as if metabolic detox is a bank account you draw from with each drinking session. The sad truth for seasoned, aging drinkers is that our bodies can't cover the transaction without overdrawing.

This realization, unlike the alcohol, is sobering. It also reminds us why it's important to develop mindful drinking habits as Father Time creeps up. If we don't, the pain will get increasingly worse.

Bright Spots

Ready for a win? For whatever reason, alcohol has been associated with lower risks of both kidney cancer and lymphoma and doesn't impact ovarian, lung, or bladder cancers.[33] Even if we keep drinking—or if the damage is already done—we'll still breathe and pee okay. I'll take it.

Finally, I want to point out that changing our behavior can make a difference. One prominent study published in the *International Journal of Cancer* showed that cutting back on alcohol lowered the risks of liver cancer significantly. In other words, participants who moderated their drinking had lower instances of liver cancer than those who kept drinking heavily.[34]

I bring this study up to make an important point: **We can impact our future health by changing what we do today, regardless of our past.** What we do from here on matters.

Recapping the Risks and Rewards

The previous two chapters have given us a framing of alcohol's two-faced nature. On one side, there are real and tangible benefits to drinking. These include friendship, creativity, earnings, and romantic relationships. On the other side lie the risks to our physical and mental health. They shouldn't be quickly dismissed; some are potentially fatal. No activity is worth missing out on months and even years of life.

But here's the good news: **we can *minimize* our health risks by embracing habits of moderation.** In other words, drinking *can* be compatible with an overall healthy lifestyle. If we're successful, we can tip the scale in favor of alcohol's benefits and away from its costs.

Our first step to getting there is to contemplate our relationship with alcohol, including why we drink, when we drink, and how much. This is where mindfulness comes in, and that's where we're headed in the next chapter.

Chapter Summary

- Alcohol's most **prominent risks** include poor choices, various cancers, heart disease, poor sleep, mental health issues, and weight gain.

- Among all cancers, alcohol's impact on **breast cancer** risks is especially notable. Breast cancer risks are already significant for many women, and even 1 daily drink causes significant increases to these risks.

- The physical effects of alcohol are met with counter-reactions from your body, which include **stimulants** and hormones like **cortisol**. This disrupts sleep patterns, induces stress and anxiety, and possibly depression.

- Alcohol stops you from burning fat and is full of empty calories. This, combined with the hormone imbalances, induces **weight gain**.

- Fortunately, moderate drinking *is not* closely linked with weight gain.

Chapter 6

Why Mindfulness Works

Awareness as a Tool

"Stay busy, get plenty of exercise, and don't drink too much. Then again, don't drink too little."

Herman Smith-Johannsen

Researchers at University College London gathered 70 high-risk drinkers to learn how mindfulness affected consumption. They split participants into two groups, with each receiving one of two tools for handling cravings—mindfulness training or relaxation techniques.

Mindfulness training was described as "ultra-brief", meaning it was short and simple. But it emphasized being "aware of feelings and bodily sensations.[1]" They then observed how the participants drank the following week.

The results were compelling. A week later, they found that both groups experienced less cravings, but **only the mindfulness group successfully cut their intake**. The average drop was roughly 5 weekly servings (9 units in the UK).

Another study, this time out of Seattle, looked at the long-term effects of mindfulness in recovery programs.[2] This time there were 3 treatment options: standard therapy, relapse avoidance, and mindfulness training. Like the London study, the results were attention-grabbing:

- Compared to standard therapy, mindfulness training led to a

59% cut in heavy drinking.

- At 6 months, the mindfulness group reported **31% fewer** heavy drinking days versus standard therapy.

- At 12 months, the mindfulness group was the **least likely** to engage in heavy drinking *at all*, and by significant proportions.

- They concluded that mindfulness had "a more enduring effect" than the other treatment programs.

This chapter is about shedding light on these studies. We've learned what alcohol does to our bodies and the array of benefits and risks. It's time to pivot our focus to mindfulness as a solution. Why is mindfulness an appropriate tool for us? How can it help us control our drinking, change our behaviors, and improve our lives?

The first thing to do is come to an understanding of what mindfulness is. As I mentioned in the Introduction, this isn't easy. As a term, mindfulness is everywhere. When something becomes common, it's subject to wide interpretation, which then leads to confusion.

I'm going to give you a minimalist interpretation of what mindfulness is. From there, we'll explore why mindfulness is an ideal path for reforming drinking habits.

Mindfulness 101

Mindfulness, in its essence, means **coming back to the present moment**. The primary benefit of presence is **awareness**. This opens a door to what's called **interoception,** which is our ability to interpret signals from the body. In any given moment, and with a little effort, we can become more cognizant of *what* we're experiencing and *why* we feel the way we do, simply by being more connected with our bodily sensations.

Drinkers can use this awareness to better understand **why** they drink, **when** they drink, and **how much**. This simple change—**becoming more aware of our bodies, feelings, and servings**—is *our* definition of mindfulness.

Being "aware" sounds easy. But it's as if we're neurologically wired in the opposite direction. Instead of focusing on *now*, we replay the past, fantasize about the future, and daydream. Wellness enthusiasts have come to revere mindfulness as a remedy for these distractions. But today's distractions, which are on demand and in the palms of our hands, are challenging enemies.

Don't get it twisted, I enjoy my technology as much as the next person. My inner minimalist wants to dump everything and survive by Google Pixel alone. But the pull of screens is powerful. They suck us into dependency, eventually doing as much harm as they do good. Does this problem sound familiar yet?

It's important to view modern distractions and alcohol for what they are: **comforts**. Our devices comfort us when stillness is too unsettling, quickly giving us a curated world where we feel connected and entertained. Alcohol is similar, comforting us when sobriety becomes painful. Like our phones, it carries us away to another place.

The point is that alcohol is another agent in our culture of distraction. The path goes like this:

1. Life, in various ways, is **uncomfortable.**

2. Alcohol becomes an **escape** from discomfort, but can become risky.

3. To avoid the risk, we must **limit** the role of alcohol.

4. We can do this with **mindful awareness** of why we drink, when, and how much.

Simply put, we drink to avoid the discomfort of the moment—anxiety, stress, boredom, whatever. It's okay in moderation. But this can get complicated in a big hurry. When that happens, alcohol stops relieving discomfort and becomes a revolving door of suffering.

Fortunately, we can unhinge the revolving door by **becoming aware** of how it got there. This involves seriously contemplating our relationship with alcohol, then re-imagining it entirely. Mindfulness will be a critical tool we can consistently turn to along the way.

Mindfulness and Moderation

Let's go back to the London and Seattle studies. Together, they showed us the impact of mindfulness on drinking patterns. The London study proved that mindfulness doesn't have to be complicated to have impact. The Seattle study corroborated those results, while also revealing that mindfulness has long-term staying power.

Both studies admitted they couldn't be sure why mindfulness made a difference. One explanation suggests being mindful activates the parasympathetic nervous system, which has a calming effect. Another version says being mindful helps us experience cravings in a new way. Instead of being overwhelmed, we can view them as temporary feelings that will fade with time.

There's probably no single mechanism driving the effectiveness of mindfulness. Broader studies have shown that it changes the structure and function of the brain[3], including increased gray matter in areas that control decision-making. Furthermore, regular practice decreases matter in the parts that control fight or flight. You might imagine that this brings a host of physical and mental health benefits, including decreases in cortisol[4], relief from chronic pain, and mediation of depression and anxiety[5].

In short, **mindfulness alters our experience of discomfort**. Remember: Escaping discomfort is a key driver of our drinking habits. This being the case, tolerating discomfort is a critical skill for living a damp lifestyle.

Imagine the improvements you'd see with better management of stress and anxiety, for example. Or the ability to recognize an alcohol craving as thirst and dehydration. Would this not have immense impact on your relationship with alcohol? With any luck, you'll come to accept discomfort as a normal part of work life, home life, or sharing a one-sink master bathroom. (Life advice: You'll never win against a curling iron.)

In any case, mindfulness has been repeatedly shown to **help people manage cravings and cut back**. This is what the London and Seattle participants experienced—a cluster of new powers they found in mindfulness techniques. They were better able to spot triggers, manage cravings, and embrace discomfort. All because they became *aware*.

It's worth noting that these powers aren't exclusive to drinkers. Smokers, binge eaters, and even porn addicts have benefited from these techniques. Whatever our habit, we can take control with mindfulness and interoception, which are the paths to understanding what we're doing and why.

Cultivating Mindfulness

Acquiring new skills is kinda like learning to juggle. If you overcomplicate it with too many balls in the air, you'll stumble and become frustrated. A simple approach—one or two balls—is wise.

This is similar to the tiny habits approached popularized by BJ Fogg, who showed us that small changes work wonders. The London study showed that simplicity and success are closely connected. Let's follow their lead and keep mindfulness simple.

So here's the deal: No mandatory meditation sessions. No need for perfect breathing techniques. No demands to become the Dalai Lama. Instead, you're going to focus your efforts on 4 tweaks to your current routine:

1. Shutting off **autopilot**.

2. Noticing bodily **sensations**, **feelings**, and **thoughts**.

3. Recognizing and accepting **discomfort**.

4. Being mindful of **triggers**.

Each of these practices will help you become more aware, either of yourself or your environment.

Autopilot, for example, is the zombie-like state you enter during routine behaviors, like your daily commute for the 600th time. Shutting it off is critical for being connected to your body and surroundings, which is how you'll become aware of sensations and discomforts. Only then will you understand what's behind your habits. Otherwise, it'll be harder to shed light on them to make the changes you're hoping for.

Of course, it's never a bad time to practice any of these skills. But for our purposes they're especially important when alcohol is present or we're experiencing a craving. After all, it's how we feel when we're drinking (or about to) that we're most concerned with.

The last several chapters have set the stage for our journey to mindful drinking habits. We've learned what alcohol does to our body, the assorted benefits of drinking, and the many liabilities. We've also discovered why mindfulness is an excellent tool for reforming our relationship with alcohol.

With that background in place, we can now move on to Part 2 on getting ready. In this next part, we're going to find your core motivations for cutting back and dig into habit science. Once that's done, we'll jump into Part 3 on planning and execution.

Chapter Summary

- **Mindfulness** is about bringing yourself back to the present moment. The main benefit is **awareness**.

- Mindfulness will help you to become more aware of your **body**, your **feelings**, and your **servings**. In other words, you'll become aware of **when** you drink, **why** you drink, and **how much**.

- Alcohol functions as a distraction and an escape from **discomfort**. In excess, it stops relieving discomfort and becomes a source of suffering.

- Studies have shown that mindfulness is a **useful tool** for managing cravings and reducing alcohol intake. They have also shown that mindfulness training *does not* have to be complicated to have impact.

- The positive impact of mindfulness most likely comes from two sources; 1) changes to the way we experience **discomfort**; 2) helping us interpret signals from our body (**interoception**).

Exercise 2

Shutting Off Autopilot

BACKGROUND: Autopilot is the zombie-like state your brain goes into when you're going through the motions of daily life. The brain does this as part of its consistent love affair with efficiency, regularly dispatching anything routine to the land of unconscious habits. It's something about your brain you can appreciate, as I discuss in Chapter 8.

But autopilot can also take you out of the present moment, making you entirely unaware of what you're doing and why. Shutting off autopilot is a good start to being mindful and present.

WHAT TO DO: There is a detailed exercise in the **free workbook**, which you can download at the **book's hub**. It's a 7-minute meditation exercise, which goes like this:

- Step 1: Quick body scan (1-2 min.)

- Step 2: Pay attention to your environment (1-2 min.)

- Step 3: Focus on your breathing (2-3 min.)

- Step 4: Reflection and notes

This simple exercise will show you how to take your brain off autopilot, become aware of your bodily sensations, and be present. If you already have a meditation practice in your life, you're aware of the process and its benefits. If you don't have experience with meditation, it might sound a little...granola, I guess.

But it's a skill that will serve you well when you're learning to identify and manage alcohol cravings, which are the powerful brain messages that tell us it's time for a drink. Learning to manage cravings with mindfulness is an important part of this journey.

Part 2: Getting Ready

Chapter 7

The Importance of Motivation

Finding Your "Why"

"When you've got a dream, you've got to grab it and never let go."

Carol Burnett

When alcohol releases dopamine from the pleasure center, you get a surge of euphoria that's recorded by your brain. An association is quickly made between alcohol and joy, forming the basis of the "alcohol-reward cycle." That cycle becomes a trail of breadcrumbs you repeatedly follow, like Hansel and Gretel, back to alcohol's gingerbread house.

Each time you follow the trail of alcohol rewards, the intention is obvious: another nibble of euphoria. This means, as of today, that you are *highly* motivated to drink. You like the taste, revel in the high, and find quick comfort in a cocktail. You're not alone—we all do. It's a marker of the habit.

To your credit, you're now ready to pare down the servings. The problem is you have to flip the motivation circuit in the opposite direction. If you really think about it, this is a hairpin turn, since your goal is to turn today's yum into tomorrow's yuck. How do you put a hard stop on motivation, make a U-turn, and drive it in the opposite direction?

The short answer, as Michael Levy suggested, is by **overcoming ambivalence**—the existence of competing, contradictory feelings living in your head at the same time.[1] Ambivalence is entirely normal when you're trying to reform habits. Right now, for example, you're motivated to drink *and* want to cut back at the same time. These are competing goals at odds with one another.

Getting past this quandary requires finding a **clear set of motivations** for adopting healthier habits. In habit science, these motivations are called your *why*. Just thinking it's good for you isn't enough—you have to tease out your true desires, something you crave for your future. Otherwise, you'll be ambivalent about changing your behavior and more likely to fall back into old habits.

My why, like many other parents, started with a little girl.

The Origins of My Why

Before committing to Susie, my spouse, I pretty much worked, dated, and socialized. I'd do other things here and there to seem well-rounded—swing golf clubs, the occasional rec sport, read high-brow books, and watch low-brow movies. But life was mostly about dating people, meeting people, and pretending to know things. (What else would a professor do?)

Other times, I'd retreat to equally satisfying alone time. It was a period of life in which I had freedom, control, and a healthy balance between peace and commotion.

What I love about Susie is that we are, in many ways, birds of a feather. She's also a social creature who works to develop relationships, maybe too hard. Then she toils at work, *definitely* too hard. (I feel like a bedtime story at her house was excerpts from *The Protestant Work Ethic*.)

Despite the excesses, I dug all of it. She was a fun, charismatic achiever with full lips and a well-behaved dog. The package, as they say. (Tragically, the dog is now crotchety and defiant.)

I quickly learned that we shared a penchant for social drinking. In fact, our first date was at a tavern, an informal lunch-and-beer rendezvous. I was relieved because, like most daters, I firmly believed that my chances spiked when the drinks were spiked.

> Drink this in: 86% of daters drink alcohol on dates, while 37% admit to drinking *before* a date.[2] If it goes horribly wrong, 100% drink after a date.

Susie and I merrily canoodled around town, enjoying casual dinners, bottles and corks, and a little footsie. This led to more intimate get-to-gethers at her place, where I'd always show up with a bottle in hand.

It's not that we *always* drank. But the odds were 2 to 1 in favor of intoxication over sobriety. With time, we developed a relationship habit: wine with dinner, happy hours, reverse happy hours, and cold beers on hot patios—an ongoing game of Just the Tipsy.

Just as we were getting ready to move in together, Susie made a surprise visit to my apartment with a small gift bag in hand. My mind percolated. Was it a smart watch? A pair of Ray-Ban Clubmasters? Spiked Mint Chocolate Chip Ice Cream by Tipsy Scoop? (I'm being really specific for a reason—please buy me a tub of that.)

My eager hand dove into the bag to find...a pregnancy test. More precisely, a Clearblue digital pregnancy test with SmartCountdown technology (patent pending). No lines, no guessing, just plain English: PREGNANT. My inner monologue opted for just plain Spanish: *hijo de puta*. Then French: *fils de pute*. Then Bengali: .

"But we're too old!" I blurted, like I was just offered KidzBop live tickets. (We were 37 at the time. She insists I was being ridiculous, but time will vindicate me.) Thankfully, I went through all five stages of grief in seven minutes and adjusted my response to the news.

"What about Argentina?" I asked, hoping our trip to Argentine wine country wasn't dead to rights. It was. And still is today.

My dating-to-pregnancy experience with Susie bore a strange resemblance to my alcohol-drenched social life. In both cases, alcohol was added early—at times, to excess—until eventually becoming a fixture. In a nutshell, alcohol became common, then expected, then habitual.

With parenthood looming, however, a big reckoning was on the horizon. That reckoning would become my core motivation to change my relationship with alcohol.

Along Came June

I don't usually frame my life in Miley Cyrus lyrics, but my first daughter came in like a wrecking ball.

Susie went into labor at 35 weeks, meaning baby June would start her life in a neonatal intensive care unit (NICU). Right about the time I came to terms with this, the contractions swarmed the room.

The moans were bestial, which the nurse explained was common with back labor. Apparently, June was shoving her head into Susie's spine, which I've read is like being stabbed in the back with a hot poker. (Hindsight: Thus began the still-raging mother-daughter wars.)

The epidural was late and toothless. Never has a "painkiller" caused so much anguish and such little relief. Somewhere in the fog, I realized "birth plan" was a top-shelf oxymoron, right up there with "living dead" and "humane slaughter."

After a grueling crescendo, the chaos turned into joy. There was June, belting out the hoarse cry of a newborn while her mom and dad teared up in wonder. (Susie was also *literally* torn up. But that's her story to tell.)

The NICU nurses looked over June and attached the mass of wires she'd wear for the next three weeks. A little cuddle time, a few pictures, and off she went in an incubator. I had abruptly become a father. And yet all I could muster in my brain were two selfish thoughts: *I'm hungry* and *I could really use a drink.*

After some gentle reassurance from the NICU people, Susie and I left June to go rest in the postpartum room. We talked for a bit, mostly sharing our bewilderment with the whole thing. It's funny how confused you can be by predictable events. We were in the place we planned to be in after the thing we'd been waiting for. Why were we so baffled?

A 90 second pause in the conversation sent Susie into a well-earned slumber. There I sat in a quiet hospital room, next to my comatose baby momma, for all intents and purposes alone.

I'm usually okay with alone time, which explains the book writing. But on this occasion it felt different, probably because I was riding high on freshly minted fatherhood. The unlikely combination of solitude and energy was odd, unsettling even. Then came the tug, the return of a thought from earlier—*how about that drink?*

Google Maps confessed that there was a bar just down the street. It was called The Usual, ironically appropriate since my night had been anything but. So I left Susie to her recovery sleep and ambled down to the watering hole, allegedly to celebrate a new life but really in the hopes of finding an ear to bend.

Some of the details have faded, but I remember the bartender's initial tone was perfunctory—"How's your night going?", "What'll it be?", that line of questioning. I played coy at first, unsure if the barkeep and lone patron would find my night harrowing enough for a screen break. I spotted a bottle of Basil Hayden's on the shelf, so I ordered an Old Fashioned. (Dads gotta keep it classy.) The bartender went to work while I sat in quiet reflection.

Drink in hand, I tried to organize my mind as I let the ice melt a bit. Then I took my first "Happy birthday to June" sips. I'm not sure if my face looked proud or overwhelmed, but something made the bartender extend a conversational olive branch. He asked again—this time with genuine interest in his voice—what I was up to that night.

"My baby girl was just born over at Baylor," I said, with as much modesty as I could muster.

His face lit up. "Heyyyy! Congrats!"

The guy three seats down, looking about 30 years old but 60 years bored, was more subdued. But he smiled and repeated the sentiment. I expressed my gratitude just before regaling them with the wilder parts, an oral Yelp review of the birthing experience. About the time I got done describing the NICU, the barkeep offered me a shot on the house.

"Tonight, I'll definitely take you up on that," I said enthusiastically. I hadn't planned on slamming liquor, but this was no occasion for being rude. (Disclaimer: That's what I always say when I accept free shots.) He mixed this with that while telling me he had a girl himself. She was five.

"There's nothing like having a girl," he said. He believed that the father-daughter bond was truly special, a new frontier of human love.

I'd heard such ramblings countless times before, of course. But they suddenly seemed less mundane.

The bartender finished his charity work and served up three shots, one for each of us. What came out was yellow enough to assume that pineapple was involved, a mixer I don't love. But it seemed uncouth to ask penetrating questions, so I just clinked and drank. (Yep, definitely pineapple.)

The three of us sat and talked, mostly about parenting, but a little about how life changes in general. The barkeep told me that things would never be the same, almost entirely for the better. He confessed that the arrival of his daughter had helped him see himself differently, to work on being better and making her proud.

I never discovered exactly what "making her proud" meant for him. I like to think he funded a law degree with his bartending money from The Usual, then helped exonerate falsely convicted felons before taking his little girl to watch them reunite with lost families. But he probably just bought her a Polly Pocket.

Anyway, we talked long enough for an Old Fashioned, a free shot, and then a second Old Fashioned. By then, it was time to prance back to the postpartum room. Fortunately, I wasn't missed while I was gone. Sadly, that hasn't happened again since.

***

In a sense, my moderation journey started in that bar. I just didn't realize it at the time. I couldn't yet fathom how my daily life was about to change.

The way I slept.

The way I socialized.

The hours I kept.

The wake-up alarms I'd no longer need.

The shirts I'd buy to replace the spit-up.

The forlorn goodbyes to selfish pursuits.

The wine I wouldn't taste.

The beer I wouldn't pour.

The high-end cocktails I'd never order.

The trappings of parenting and its discontents.

It would all become part of the package.

People often describe their first child's birth as the best day of their life. I'll admit I'm not so sure. Five years in—and now with two girls—I imagine it could run second to the day they move out.

Here's what I *am* sure of: other than your own birth and death, no single event will change you more. On Monday, you're living the ego-centric freedom of childlessness. By close of business Tuesday, you're the indentured servant of a tiny, extremely cute human. Quinceañeras, bar mitzvahs, graduations, weddings—none of them can hold a candle to an infant.

Like I said, Miley Cyrus nailed it. (What are the odds?) It was just a matter of time until that wrecking ball *really* broke my walls.

Susie's Perspective

If *my* world was turned upside down, Susie's was obliterated. The breastfeeding was only the beginning. She made milk with her body and snuck it through tiny holes to an infant who wasn't decent enough to say "Thank you." (And still hasn't.) I watched the whole thing with rapt attention, first out of wonder. Then wonder turned into sheer respect.

For those who don't know, most newborns eat every 90 minutes. But the clock starts at the *beginning* of a feeding. Each feeding runs about a half hour, leaving an hour break between feedings. That's why Susie looked so worn down—she was having her nipples mangled 16 hours a day. Yet somehow, she was still beautiful! (Saved it. Also, call your mom.)

To find a semblance of freedom—and maybe a sprinkle of wine—Susie had to produce supply. But to produce supply, she had to pump. Which brings us to the pumping. Oh, the pumping. I can still hear the monotonous rhythm of motor-driven suction.

Using the wrong-sized nipple adapter, called a *flange*, made Susie's nipples look like they'd fallen out of a moving car. And finding the right-sized flange was like panning for gold. I still have images in my head of Susie asleep with flanges suctioned to her beleaguered nipples, trickles of yellow-tinged breast milk crawling into a Medela cup.

We were Medela people. I know, because my job was to wash all the Medela parts with a Medela brush and Medela steam bags. (**Quick financial advice:** Invest in Medela.)

For her trouble, Susie got advice from pretty much everywhere. Most of it was outdated, repetitive, or flat-out wrong. The more she read, the worse she felt. By some accounts, she was "failing" by not gushing gallons of milk like a prized cow. Others said she was a shit mother for supplementing with formula, which in some circles is like putting your baby in a tanning bed.

It wasn't all bad, of course. But breastfeeding is a prime example of a new thing that necessitates a new you. The larger point is that **life disruptions come in different forms.** Mine were June and fatherhood. Susie's were June, motherhood, breastfeeding, breast pumping, recovery, and the Family and Medical Leave Act. Different people's worlds change in different ways.

Maybe *your* June was a corporate ladder to climb. Or the financial realities of home ownership. It could be that an aging parent got sick, or your own health took a dive. What matters is that something sparked a new desire in you, a drive to contemplate your relationship with alcohol. In the next exercise, you're going to pin down—as specifically as possible—what those reasons are and why you're here.

Don't forget that the reason you need a solid set of motivations to drink mindfully is because you're current habit is to drink mindlessly. Those mindless reflexes are solid and won't budge without good cause. This stubbornness, as we'll learn in the next chapter, is the nature of habits.

Chapter Summary

- All drinkers, thanks to alcohol's intoxicating chemistry, are **motivated to drink**. This is especially problematic when we need to be motivated in the opposite direction.

- **Overcoming ambivalence** is key to flipping motivation back in your favor.

- Finding your **why**—a clear set of motivations for change—is a great way to overcome feelings of ambivalence.

Exercise 3

The Why Drill

BACKGROUND: By my third month of fatherhood, my drinking habits were under heavy scrutiny. Groggy late-night feedings got the moderation ball rolling. Slight hangover parenting was the clincher. Eventually, it felt like freshman year in high school—new faces, new schedule, and an impossible locker combination.

All of that delivered an epiphany: to do this new life right, I had to *want* different things. But I also needed to discover my reasons for wanting those things in the first place. I needed a "why"—a core set of motivations. To get there, I used an exercise touted by habit gurus called a **why drill.**[1]

Why drills are important because they help us narrow our focus into something authentic and motivating. Right now, for example, you have a specific **want**: a healthier relationship with alcohol. But you need to figure out your **underlying reasons** for wanting that new relationship. Seems like those reasons should come to light naturally. But it takes extra effort to discover them. Enter the why drill.

The drill is simple: Ask yourself *why* you want what you want five times. You'll start with the original thing and ask why you want it, then repeat the question five times over. I've included a structured why drill in the **free workbook**, which you can download at the book's hub.

My why drill looked like this:

> *I want to cut back on alcohol.*
> Why?
> *Because I want to be healthy.*
> Why?
> *Because I want to feel good every day.*
> Why?
> *Because I want to be productive.*
> Why?
> *Because I want to own more of my time.*
> Why?
> *Because I want to be present for my spouse and kids.*

You'll notice that I answered each "why" with a new desire—something I wanted. Then I dug deeper by asking why again and again. In just five rounds, I got past glittering generalities and into more detailed, actionable desires. In other words, I had macro-level goals before the drill, like being healthier. After the drill, I had **medium-level goals** like productivity and time.

To get even deeper, I picked a couple of my favorite answers and kept going. It went like this:

> *I want to feel good every day.*
> Why?
> *Because I want to be in a good mood.*
> Why?
> *Because I want to be more patient.*
> Why?
> *Because I want to be a better father.*
> Why?
> *Because I want to set a good example for my kids.*
> Why?
> *Because I want them to be decent people.*

Each iteration got me closer to my core, **micro-level reasons** for my goals, specific enough to be motivational *and* actionable.

I won't bore you with the next round, which basically devolved into reasons I wanted to look better naked. Just know that after two more why drills, I had a solid set of motivations for changing my drinking. In no particular order, here's what cracked the top 10:

- Getting high-quality sleep

- Having more positivity in my daily life

- Improved mood and temperament

- Playing sports and doing activities with June and April

- Taking fewer sick days

- Having less stomach fat and better skin (vanity alert)

- Maintaining libido (insecurity alert)

- Being present for family and friends

- Raising good people

- Nurturing my marriage

To do all of this, I would need to carry youthful energy into midlife and beyond. How else would I play basketball with June at 50? Or help her move the hell out of my house at 60?

Unfortunately for the happy drinker in me, alcohol would make all of it much harder. But the good news is that I became acutely aware of what *really* mattered and why I wanted to change my habits.

WHAT TO DO: Now it's your turn. Go ahead and do a couple of why drills. Again, if you want structure, go to the **book's hub** and snag the **workbook**.

Keep in mind that your why drill doesn't have to look like mine. In fact, it probably shouldn't. What we want in life is very personal. Your why could be one overarching reason, a single thing that motivates you. Or it could be a few small details that you want out of each morning. What's important is that it does justice to *your* situation and is something that drives *you*.

Within two drills, you'll have some core motivations and maybe a few peripheral ones. If you find that some aren't specific enough, just keep zooming in until it feels right. In the end, you'll have clear motivations for drinking mindfully versus mindlessly.

One last thing: Doing why drills in your head is better than not doing them at all. But writing them out will help your thinking process. Plus, your answers, which we'll use in the execution phase, will be recorded for later.

Chapter 8

Understanding Alcohol Habits

The Neurology of Mindless Drinking

habit (noun): hab•it | \ ⓍÌha-bət

1: A usual way of behaving: something that a person does often in a regular and repeated way.

2: An acquired mode of behavior that has become nearly or completely involuntary.

Merriam-Webster

Your subconscious brain can process 11 million bits of information per second. Your conscious brain, however, is limited to processing about 50.[1] This means 99.98% of what drives our behaviors is happening beneath the surface. How does your subconscious sort through so much every single second?

Part of the answer is that **it streamlines processes with habits.** When we experience something hundreds of times and get the same result, that result will be programmed into our subconscious. The more we do it, the stronger the connection and the firmer the habit.

After a few drinking episodes we acquire a perception: Alcohol relaxes us and relieves anxiety. We arrive there because the dopamine-serotonin euphoria happens immediately, while the anxiety from nerves and stimulants comes later.

In short, our subconscious makes quick connections. That's why it credits alcohol with the high but not the hangover. Our conscious mind has to make the second connection. This happens in other contexts, too. When I binge on Thin Mints, my brain makes an immediate connection with the chocolatey sugar buzz. It doesn't as quickly associate those same cookies with bloating and weight gain.

> In this way, the subconscious mind misses out on this key piece of information: that it was the alcohol that caused the feeling of anxiety in the first place. So although we can understand on a conscious level that it was the alcohol that caused the anxiety, it won't stop us from wanting a drink every time we feel anxiety or depression.
> – William Porter, *Alcohol Explained*, Chapter 2

Porter is saying that alcohol's effects on the pleasure center give us a subconscious perception that it's wonderful. It's not a false perception—the joy is real. But the pain is real, too. In our head, however, the former overrides the latter. Eventually, this results in behavioral adaptations—AKA habits—that stick.

The Power of Habits

Functionally and neurologically, **habits are shortcuts.** Our brain is in constant triage, delegating everything from breathing to language. Habits protect us from constant decision-making by putting the bulk of what we do on autopilot. So a habit's purpose is, in a word, efficiency. Probably sanity, too.

Think of your morning routine. When you wake up, you go through a set of motions: turn off your alarm, check your phone, walk to the bathroom, shower, brush your teeth, and so on.

Once in a while, something throws you off, maybe a thing isn't where it's supposed to be. (At my house, it's usually stray toys to step on.) But you typically go through the same steps unconsciously and automatically,[2] as a matter of habit. In a nutshell, **that's what a habit is**: something we do without thinking about it.

Let's imagine another wake-up scenario. Only this time, it's after a late night of binge drinking and you wake up in an unfamiliar hotel room with a random person slumbering in the bedsheets. In this scenario, there is no routine. You don't know your surroundings. You only vaguely recognize the dozing stranger.

Instead of the habitual foot drag to the bathroom, you get a different experience: a barrage of conscious decisions about each surprise you encounter, one after the other—including where the hell your pants are. That happens because what's in front of you isn't familiar and your daily habits are suspended.

The stranger in a hotel room is an especially awkward example. But the truth is that losing our habits doesn't have to be bad. In fact, it's one of the things that makes traveling so exciting. Everything is new, and novelty lights up our brain by stimulating norepinephrine.[3] But novelty is also why the same vacation can be exhausting—our habitual routines aren't there for us, so we "experience" our way to afternoon naps.

Our brain's love affair with efficiency is also why *bad* habits are stubborn. As I said before, our most habitual behaviors happen unconsciously. This means that stopping a bad habit—or building better ones—can only be done by recognizing the unconscious influences on our behavior. Mind you, this isn't a simple task. It involves digging up things from the nether regions of our minds so we can understand our behaviors.

Carl Jung wrote that "Until you make the unconscious conscious, it will direct your life and you will call it fate."

Therein lies the crowning reason why habits matter and why changing them is hard. The things we do without thinking shape our daily life—the way we work, manage our time, parent our children, eat our food, and use our cell phones—all of them are primarily driven by habits.

Changing these behaviors means doing what our brain is avoiding: *thinking* about them. But the good news is that, when we're successful, changing habits can open new doors and improve our lives.

The Basal Ganglia and Habits

In *The Power of Habit*, Charles Duhigg compares the brain to an onion. The outer layers are more developed and do complex thinking. The inside parts, closer to the brain stem, are more primitive and perform basic functions: breathing, oxygen exchange, fight-or-flight instincts, etc.

Just above your primitive brain in the center of your skull are your basal ganglia, a group of cells about the size of a golf ball. The basal ganglia are connected to the limbic system, which is responsible for focus, rewards, and the alarm response that kicks in when you're caught singing Nickelback songs.

MIT researchers discovered that rats with damaged basal ganglia had trouble performing routine tasks, like lifting a flap to get to their food. It was as if they had unlearned something that was once automatic. This prompted questions about the basal ganglia's role in habits. Time for MIT to do what they do best: torture lab rats.

When they tinkered in the lab, the research team discovered that rats in a T-shaped maze would eventually learn the path to a reward, which was a piece of chocolate. Starting in the bottom of the T, the rats would get a **trigger**: a *click* sound followed by the opening of a door. The smell of chocolate induced a **craving**, which is basically a desire to solve a problem (hunger in this case). They then **responded** by sniffing out a path.

In early runs, their movements were slow and casual, almost like they weren't putting much into it. They'd often take a wrong turn to the right, then dawdle before doubling back to find their **reward**. Just a rat walk in the rat park with a rat happy ending.

Each rodent went through the maze hundreds of times, exposing them to the same trigger (the *click*), craving (smell of chocolate), routine (maze), and reward (chocolate) until it was habit. *Click*, smell, maze, chocolate. Rinse and repeat times infinity. This sequence—trigger, craving, routine, reward—is what James Clear calls a **habit loop.**[4]

Brain scan data gave MIT their own rewards. First, they discovered that the rats' brain activity changed as they became more familiar with the process. In early runs, their brain activity was off the charts because they were working hard to make sense of things. They spent extra brain energy sorting out where they were and what they should do. But their brain activity decreased with repetition. Eventually, even the parts of the brain responsible for memory stayed at rest and the only part at work was the basal ganglia. Everything had become a habit.

Whether it's rats in a maze or styling your hair, the habit formation process is the same: trigger-craving-routine-reward. We have to try, fail, and try again until we're rewarded. But eventually the wrong movements fade and the right ones—which end in reward—stick. When they're rewarded repeatedly, they become automatic.

This conversion of a sequence of movements into an automatic routine is called **chunking**. Once the behaviors are chunked together, our brain has created a functioning habit loop.

It's important to remember that the basal ganglia run the habit show. They process our chunked behaviors and habit loops. They also function subconsciously. This is important for drinkers because it means **our drinking habits lie underneath the surface,** a set of thoughtless, chunked behaviors. In short, the details of our drinking—what we drink, how much, and why—are part of a habit loop.

With alcohol, the loop is driven by a drug with powerful reward effects. This is why it's a dangerous substance that's not just habit-forming, but also addictive. It sneaks itself deeper into our subconscious and entices us to engage the habit more frequently to reap the rewards. The more we do it, the more we want it and the more risk we take on.

In reality, a drinker's habit loop has an additional step:

drinking trigger —> alcohol craving —> drink —> reward —> *risk*

Since I'm not the best at clever names, I call this modified habit loop the **alcohol loop**. (Act impressed, I'm fragile.) To better understand our alcohol loop—and change our habits—we have to learn what sets it off and how we feel when that happens.

Make no mistake: This is an acquired skill. But we can harness it with a little effort. Our first step is **gaining awareness of our triggers.** After that, we'll learn how to **manage the cravings** that arise from those triggers.

Explaining Drinking Triggers

Every time we take a drink our brain records what happened just before—*what did I see, hear, and feel before this?* At that point, it files all of them away as **triggers**—pieces of information that tell our brain a reward is on the way.[5] For the rats it was a click. For drinkers, it's whatever surrounds our drinking experiences—places, faces, even fleeting thoughts.

With enough repetition, the neurological connection between triggers and alcohol rewards becomes solidified, until we crave alcohol every Friday at 5 PM. (You're right—3 PM.) The vast majority of this happens subconsciously, meaning we're entirely unaware of what sets off our alcohol loop.

Over the years, the most likely thing is that your triggers have expanded exponentially. Makes sense, given you have more drinking experiences with time. Each day, weekend, month, and year gives us chances to associate new places and faces with alcohol.

A new wine bar opens down the street. A budding friendship grows at the local pub. Or the new job comes with "optional" gatherings that feature fully stocked bars. If you live in the Western world and leave your house, there are always fresh opportunities to find triggers.

To illustrate, let's go back over my own drinking story from the introduction, only this time through the lens of drinking triggers:

- In my original tween binge, when I was 12, the first trigger was good old-fashioned **boredom**, closely followed by childlike **curiosity**.

- In high school, I added **social** gatherings and friends to my triggers—places and faces.

- In college, I added social networking, friend bonding, and sports, both watching *and* playing.

- In the high-stress grad school years, I added academic **anxiety**, financial worries, and job market strain.

- In the life-building years, I added dating, career **stress**, and **parenting** exhaustion.

Two things are worth close attention. First, notice the common triggers shared by most drinkers: boredom, curiosity, social life, anxiety, and stress, among others. Second, in each phase of life, you'll notice that I added new triggers. By grad school, it wasn't just places and faces that triggered drinking, but also moods and emotions.

Even the experience of having a family didn't stop me from amassing new triggers. In fact, I can think of four recently added triggers as I type: two feral children, plumbing issues, and the sound of Susie opening a bottle of Bonanza. Just with those I'm all triggered up for a while.

Here's the takeaway: Frequent drinkers steadily amass triggers over time. We begin to associate drinking with more places, faces, and feelings. On the flip side, we rarely (if ever) throw a trigger out with the trash. Just look at me. I now have more triggers than an NRA convention. And every single one of them sets off the alcohol loop.

Now, I can't take all the credit for my library of triggers. In recent years, our society has opened up the floodgates of alcohol. This has only made it easier to stockpile triggers and harder to control our servings.

Society and Alcohol Triggers

Today, once we reach legal age, alcohol is easier to get than ever before. It's also been normalized in places where it was previously a faux pas. These changes have ushered in a golden era of access, which gives us ample opportunity to add more and more triggers. The reason is simple: The ubiquity of alcohol means we associate more places with drinking, thus increasing the number of triggers that set off the alcohol loop.

In the U.S., Colorado is a good example of this trend. When I moved there in August 2007 to start my master's, I thought I'd be walking into a beer drinker's paradise—lagers and ales freely flowing from public fountains and such.

To my surprise, I discovered that grocery stores could only sell low-alcohol near beer, liquor stores had banker's hours, and last call was at 12:45, ironically making it easier to get weed than alcohol by 1 AM. Turned out the Rockies had more rules than Hammurabi.

Over the next decade, however, the drinking landscape transformed. It started with grocery stores, which finally achieved their full alcohol potential.[6] Soon after, beer and wine licenses became the norm at movie theaters.

Then things really took off when the Colorado legislature legalized "common consumption areas," which are shared spaces where you can take your drink for an open-air stroll.[7] This steady push to increase alcohol's presence never stopped, as it gradually found its way into more public spaces.

The loosening of Colorado's top button reflected a gradual but perceptible American trend. State and city governments, eternally revenue-starved, started to see sin taxes as an untapped source of funds. The result was the dampening of dry counties and the expansion of retail licensing,[8] even in traditionally conservative areas.

Texas, for example, had 30 dry counties in 2009. By late 2019, that number had shrunk to five.[9] So called "brunch bills," which allow Sunday sales before noon, have sprung up across the American South, finally giving priests access to Carlo Rossi by communion time.

Out west, Mormon Utah slowly removed the stick from its bottle top, ditching its long-standing Zion Curtain law and loosening grocery store restrictions.[10] Even Disneyland, whose regulations used to rival Pakistan's, quadrupled the Magic Kingdom's liquor licenses in 2016.[11]

As alcohol has become more available, it has predictably ferreted into more places. I can hardly remember alcohol being offered at the movies when I was growing up—just over-buttered popcorn, Coke products, and Junior Mints. (Things weren't all bad, were they?)

But in the early 2000s, beer and wine crept into theaters. It was subtle at first, fun novelties at certain venues. But it became increasingly conspicuous until finally being normalized. Today, I practically de-mand a refund if MacGuffins is closed. Just like that, a new trigger is born.

The movies were just the beginning. These days, grocery stores let us sip and shop, artisan fairs have beer tents, and soccer moms hide hard seltzers in coozies. (Nobody's fooled.)

Covid-19 was the nail in the coffin for temperance advocates. The pandemic coerced state governments into looser laws, including al-cohol-to-go, delivery, and off-premise sales. These measures stuck even after the dust settled on the virus. Today, wherever you live, alcohol is as ever-present as it's ever been. And each new venue potentially adds a new trigger to our growing list.

Keep in mind that triggers alone aren't enough to drive our habits—they're just signals. But whenever a trigger rears its head, we experience **the driving force behind our habits: cravings.**

By making alcohol more available, society has made it easier to give in to cravings than it was 15 years ago. And since a big part of moderation is fighting cravings, we have our work cut out for us.

Cheetos: A Craving Story

In 2007, Cheetos were in trouble. Goldfish and Cheez-Its were cutting into their market share and outpacing their media buys. Worse yet, America's childhood obesity problem forced Frito-Lay to abandon a 60-year-long ad campaign geared at children. Seeking a solution to both problems, the snack maker moved to do something improbable: rehabilitate Cheetos by targeting the adult consumer.

It turns out that bringing a fading product back into its glory days is a massive undertaking. Frito-Lay kicked in $30 million a year on the science of irresistibility.[12] The right crunch was developed by using a $40,000 chewing robot that helped them discover the perfect break point of a Cheeto. (Fun fact: it's 4 pounds per square inch.)

They also introduced "vanishing caloric density," which tricks the brain into thinking that melting foods are calorie-neutral, so you keep eating. The addictive clincher was to throw in some MSG, which adds zero flavor but activates glutamate receptors in our taste buds.[13] In the end, they delivered what one food scientist called "one of the most marvelously constructed foods on the planet, in terms of pleasure."[14]

And yet even with all of those improvements and the dollars they'd spent, they still lacked something critical: an advertising angle. So they turned to a market research firm called NeuroFocus, whose pop neuroscience techniques delivered a strange conclusion: People secretly liked licking the dusty residue that Cheetos left behind.[15]

Cheeto lovers wouldn't admit it openly, almost as if licking snack dust was a trigger for Catholic guilt. It took brain scans to reveal the rebellious pleasure of orange fingers. But it was undeniably there. A light bulb went on: turn the glorious mess into a selling point. That's how Frito-Lay went from selling to kids to appealing to the kid in you.

What transpired from there was an award-winning ad campaign that spiked sales by 14% while rebranding the product as a fun adult snack.[16] So smashing was the campaign's success that the dust got an official name in 2020. By now, most junk foodies would sooner suck a garbage man's fingers than let any "Cheetle" go to waste. Frito-Lay even expanded the theme into the "finger-lick" Super Bowl ads that became an overnight sensation.

How did they do it? How did they successfully target a new audience, remake their product, *and* increase their market share at the same time? By designing an ad campaign that capitalized on the power of **cravings.**

The Power of Alcohol Cravings

A good craving doesn't just make us want something—it manipulates our behavior by making us think we can't go without it. This is why advertisers focus on a product's habit-forming qualities, like the cool feeling in a shampoo, the freshness of toothpaste, or the well-defined crunch in a Cheeto. The more powerful the craving, the less likely we are to resist it.

The problem for drinkers is that our cravings are especially potent, right up there with cigarettes and third trimester pickle sandwiches. The reason is that they can be traced back to a drug that our brain associates with euphoria and relaxation. It's also why the word "craving" is commonly used in addiction circles, where people use it to describe their most powerful urges to relapse.

A **craving** is basically **the desire to address a problem.** When we're in ear shot of someone who says the word "brunch," we suddenly have a sobriety problem. But we're not craving the mimosa itself. We're craving the *feelings* we get when we drink the mimosa. This being the case, an **alcohol craving** is best described as **a desire to feel the effects of alcohol**. The lack of alcohol will remain a problem until we give in, wait it out, or distract ourselves with something else.

Seasoned drinkers have amassed triggers over time. The result is that alcohol cravings are consistent and possibly constant. This is one of the reasons why changing our drinking behavior is hard—repeated cravings test our self-control. It's like going to the mall when you're cutting carbs and repeatedly walking past Cinnabon. By the fourth lap, you're ready to draw up terms for an unconditional surrender.

Alcohol's potency is also why moderation, for many of us, is more complicated than just drinking less. It's about identifying triggers and managing cravings. What places, faces, and situations instantly set off our alcohol loop? When are those feelings especially irresistible?

Once we identify our triggers—especially the ones lurking in our subconscious—we'll be ready to deal with the cravings they set off.

Chapter Summary

- **Habits** are neurological shortcuts that exist so our brain can maximize efficiency. These are the things we do automatically, without thinking.

- A **habit loop** is a neurological sequence consisting of 4 parts—trigger, craving, routine, and reward.

- An **alcohol loop** is the sequence that undergirds our drinking habits—drinking trigger, alcohol craving, drink, reward, risk.

- **Triggers** are bits of information that tell our brain a reward is near. **Alcohol triggers** tell us that it's time to reap alcohol rewards with a drink.

- A **craving** is the desire to address a problem. By extension, an **alcohol craving** is a desire to feel the effects of alcohol.

- Given their role in alcohol habits, **knowing your triggers** and **managing cravings** are critical for mindful moderation.

Exercise 4

Spotting Your Triggers

BACKGROUND: Spotting triggers is hard because they're **subtle** and **subconscious**. By connecting them with **cravings**, however, our brain gives us a way to sniff them out. Being successful at changing our habits means finding the places and situations where we're driven to consume.

Mind you, since we're talking about moderation and not quitting, there's no onus to completely rid ourselves of triggers and cravings. We just need to manage the ones that result in excessive servings.

A simple exercise for recognizing triggers and cravings is noting when you feel like having a drink. Each time you feel the urge, record it somewhere. I know, it sounds like a hassle. But it's an important step for truly understanding your relationship with alcohol.

To make this easier for you, I've created a **tracking spreadsheet** with a tab for recording triggers and cravings. You can download it at the **book's hub**. (Side note: You'll use the same sheet to track servings later.)

The sheet will help you record five important things:

1. **When** the trigger/craving happened (day and time)

2. **Where** you were

3. **What** you were feeling

4. **How powerful** the craving was

5. **Who** was around

The main goal of the sheet is to help you connect cravings with triggers by recording what was going on each time you felt the urge to drink. Save it to your phone's home screen or wherever you can quickly access it.

WHAT TO DO: To get started, reflect on your drinking over the last few weeks and build a list of each session.

Be sure to note the **when**, **where**, and **who** parts. If you can remember what you were feeling that's helpful. But it can be hard to dig up feelings from weeks past. The **tracking spreadsheet** I mentioned earlier has places for you to record all of this information.

Once that's done, keep a running log of your triggers and cravings. Tracking them as they arise is well worth the 60 seconds you'll spend each time you have a craving.

Do this with as many cravings as possible, even when the craving isn't very powerful. Don't be hard on yourself if you miss some here and there or the details aren't exact. Just try to be consistent.

PRO TIP: When it's inconvenient to pull up the sheet, send yourself a text message with the where, what, and who parts. The time will be automatically recorded.

In a few weeks, you'll have a trove of craving information that will open a window to your subconscious triggers. To give you an idea, here are a few cravings that came up a lot for me:

- Thirst, especially from poor hydration.

- The end of a long and stressful workday.

- The end of a short and stressful parenting night.

- Dining out, especially date nights without kids.

- Dining out, especially family meals with kids.

- Dining out, especially by myself. (A theme emerges.)

- Going to the movies.

- Sporting events or concerts.

- Susie having a drink. (This one's complicated.)

- Our couch, combined with one of the following: Netflix, Apple TV, Hulu, or HBO Max. (Stay sober for Peacock or Fubo. Not worth it.)

I had some revelations when I did this find-your-triggers exercise. For example, I found that my triggers pretty commonly popped up between 8 and 8:30 PM. This is the half-hour following our girls' bedtime. (The plot thickens.) These cravings were especially strong when our girls brought cocaine home from daycare. Eventually, I made a connection: unruly kids at bedtime triggered a craving. The underlying trigger was **parenting stress.**

After recording more triggers, I discovered a common thread: cravings were often attached to situations where I lacked control. This was how I learned that successful moderation meant getting better about accepting that which I can't control. Otherwise, stress drinking would become a thorn. There's a huge bonus here: you can get to know your triggers *and* make holistic improvements at the same time.

Some of the most important situations to record are the ones that lead to excess. Now, you probably won't write those down since intoxication hates homework. But the next day, when you're reveling in your sluggishness, record what you can. This will tell you what's happening when the off switch disappears. Knowing this will be critical in the planning and execution phase.

A great way to spotlight your cravings is to do an extended break, like Dry January or Sober October. In a month's time (or more) you're likely to experience most of your key cravings. This will allow you to attach many of them to triggers. From there, you'll have plenty of fodder for reflection. Extended breaks are an important part of this process, which is why I talk about them in detail in Chapter 16.

Of course, you don't have to take an extended break to do this exercise. Susie, for one, doesn't find those hard commitments helpful. When I boldly take a pledge, she's supportive. But she always reserves the option to have a glass. Choose your own adventure according to your situation. It's just one option.

Finally, remember that right now you're just getting information about triggers and cravings. You don't have to fight them or abstain from having a drink. We'll do that later. Of course, if you feel like cutting down now, don't let the flow of this book stop you. There's no better time than the present.

Interlude

This Is 40

"Spring reminds us that resilience is only a season away."
Angie Weiland-Crosby

I wish I could say that my path to moderation was straight and flat. But the truth is that it was snaky and bumpy. It took me *at least* two honest tries to solidify better habits. After June was born and I grew into parenthood, I had a good why to motivate myself. With that ace up my sleeve, I learned about servings, triggers, cravings, and risks with the best of intentions.

To my credit, things went well for a while. I met my goals, trimmed servings to the moderate standard, made binges rare, and started seeing positive changes in my body. Things got even brighter when we learned Susie was pregnant with our second child. As her stomach grew, so did my list of motivations for being healthier.

But I was about to get a reminder from life that habits cut both ways. Some changes motivate you to build positive habits; others send you tumbling into crisis and strip you of your progress. Just as I approached a milestone birthday, I was about to get a dose of change that I'd never fathomed. And that change would put heavy drinking back at center stage.

A New Life and a Novel Virus

Our second daughter, April, poignantly arrived one day after my 40th birthday and three weeks before the Covid-19 pandemic took hold. Her birth happened fast, almost in the front seat of Susie's CRV. (There's no experience quite like driving a woman in labor with a crowning infant.)

With the outbreak of the pandemic, normal life died as fast as April was born. Every human struggled with what the pandemic really meant. It was a slow burn, as the weight of it inched onto our shoulders each day. But by the end of March 2020, we were all engulfed in it. And it changed the way we drank.

The pandemic shackled us to our houses, canceled sports, and moved birthdays onto Zoom. No industry felt the impact of quarantine more than food and hospitality, which plunged into an existential crisis. By April 2020, bars and restaurants were more embattled than Democrats in rural Texas.

State governors, mostly under duress, threw the industry a lifeline by legalizing curbside sales, liquor to-go, and deliveries. We the people—pillars of civic duty—passionately accepted these offers.

We had plenty reason to. For some, it was the somber realization that our kids, now fully under our care, were assholes. For others, liquor was a welcomed sedative, numbing either single's loneliness or couple's boredom. The result was a 34% increase in alcohol sales from April to June in 2020.[1]

More interesting still were the nuances of the Covid spike. The increase was higher for liquor, which grew by 49% versus beer (30%) and wine (29%). And a big chunk of sales was driven by what the industry calls "large-pack sales": boxed wine, big liquor handles, and cases of beer.[2] We all know that pandemic anxieties were tough sons-of-bitches to drown. Now we have the market statistics to back that up.

What's most impressive is that all that hooch flowed through an impromptu system of curbside service and delivery, which I'm convinced is our species' greatest feat of social engineering. Drink this in: There were no sports, no mass gatherings, and near-universal bar closures, yet there was a pronounced *increase* in consumption. My favorite part? The spike was primarily driven by young adults and people with multiple children.[3] (Go ahead, take a bow.)

Parents of pandemic teens will torch my Celica for saying this, but having little ones was especially tough. Susie and I found ourselves with two of them, one a completely dependent infant (as most infants are) and the other an attention-starved two-year-old. We suddenly had to navigate virtual workplaces and daycare closures while keeping both kids alive.

Those were long, harried days, heavy on multitasking and short on routine. On top of that, Covid's threat to infants was unclear. This meant the threshold of our front door turned into a paranoid customs zone. All our old habits, it seemed, were a bad fit for quarantine.

I found myself craving alcohol more and more, as self-medicating the stress became more attractive. The network of delivery services that our society adopted—Drizly, Instacart, and others—made it even harder to fend off cravings. Eventually, getting the kids to sleep meant it was time for Cabernet. If wine didn't sound good, I honed my Old Fashioned skills.

Susie and I kept pace with the drinking world by taking things up a full notch by summer. And I quickly found myself back in heavy drinking territory despite knowing the risks.

Six months into the pandemic the effects of alcohol were once again taking their toll. I was increasingly listless, edging out my infant daughter for the household napping title. About the same time, my first telehealth appointment produced a lipid panel with two "flags," a euphemism that means your organs are displeased.

Just like before, there was no obvious sign of alcohol trouble—no horrible diagnosis, no job issues, no interventions. But the signs—ahem, *flags*—were there. I was already feeling dips in energy, vitality, and creativity, critical intangibles for the better life I hoped for. These were joined by muscle loss and stomach fat, which Susie can confirm are *extremely* tangible.

I knew in my expanding gut that I had to bring back an old question: Did I need to quit alcohol entirely to be the best version of myself?

At first glance, my return to heavy drinking seems like a hard fail. Or maybe an admission that moderation is a fool's errand. But it's an important twist in the story because it leads to a critical lesson: **crises**

can rattle drinking habits. They're even more likely to do so if they disrupt your daily routine.

We've discussed that alcohol is a psychoactive drug that triggers our pleasure center. When our emotions are out of whack because of the external world, we need to be extra careful how we respond to triggers and cravings.

Reviving Moderation

One sign of a deeper alcohol problem is repeated attempts to change that go nowhere. When we can't meet a daily or weekly serving goal, we have to ask ourselves why our goals got away from us and what to do about it.

In my case, the pandemic had thrown off any semblance of normalcy and obliterated my serving goals—whatever moderation habits I had acquired in the preceding year had a virus of their own. It was time to ask hard questions.

Why did I return to old habits? How hard would it be to bring back mindfulness? And what would be an undeniable sign that moderation wasn't for me?

Answering the first question was easy: My drinking was a self-medicated response to the stresses and anxieties of the crisis.

Just think of the pandemic from the perspective of habit science. Habits are daily routines that are mostly subconscious. Covid-19 threw those routines in the biohazard bin. In other words, the virus made simple choices *hard* by putting threats everywhere.

Going to the grocery store? Keep your distance. Wanna go visit your mom? Better not, old people are dying. Got an Amazon package on the way? Get the oven mitts and prep the bleach wipes. The pandemic was the ultimate anti-habit, a train that barreled head-on into daily routines.

The most common human response—including my own—was acute anxiety. Again, our lessons on habits shed light on why: I didn't have my reliable go-to behaviors at my side, the routines that make daily life manageable. The mixed messaging from government, businesses, and doctors didn't help things. So there I was, sitting at home, bewildered and scared. (It did help a little bit that I got to work in sweatpants.)

I eventually got a hold on the moment and settled into a mixed routine of teaching online and taking care of April. Once I had found a semblance of normal, I went back to the alcohol literature to decide how to move forward. The most helpful wisdom was on the different types of hiccups you can have in this process, commonly called "regressions."

From least problematic to most problematic, there are 3 types: **slips, setbacks,** and **ricochets.** Here's what they mean:[4]

- A **slip** is a "minor violation" of your moderation plan. An isolated binge during a night out with friends is a good example.

- A **setback** is a return to a previous stage of change. (Quick reminder: the stages are contemplation, planning, execution, and maintenance.) If you'd been successfully *maintaining* healthier habits for a while but then had to go back to planning, you'd be in a setback.

- A **ricochet** is when drinking behavior becomes riskier than it originally was. If you originally drank 15 to 20 servings per week and that increased to 25 to 30 servings, you'd be in a ricochet.

Since it lasted a few months and mostly mirrored my drinking habits before June was born, my pandemic spike was more than a slip, but it wasn't a ricochet. I was going through a setback. I basically found myself back at the beginning, rehashing the old cut-or-quit question.

At first, I wasn't sure how bad I should feel about this. Excuses, as usual, were easy to conjure up. *This is a once-a-century health crisis and the kids are a handful—you deserve a whiskey sour.* But I was back to taking on more risks than I wanted to, which meant sacrificing my big-picture goal: a longer, healthier life.

***

I eventually learned that regressions are completely normal. The worst that can happen is we dwell on them or blame ourselves. I also learned that slips and setbacks can be easily fixed if we quickly reestablish good habits. That was comforting to read. But I still wondered how hard it would be get back to good. Would I quickly jump back to the mindful habits I had painstakingly built?

Looking back, I'm now surprised at how easy it was to reintroduce healthier drinking habits. Charles Duhigg talks about crises being ideal for taking stock and improving habits, and I certainly experienced a version of that on the alcohol front. First, I was able to get a crystal-clear view of my **most powerful triggers**: stress and anxiety. The world around you will always induce cravings. But the toughest triggers to wrangle, for me at least, are the ones from internal feelings.

These reflections ended with an important realization: **to make drinking habits "crisis-proof," I needed to focus more on systems rather than goals.** Being accountable to goals had served me well for a while. But when the world went apeshit, they didn't hold up. I had to back them up with a system that would set me up for long-term success. Once I did that, the path of moderation became much smoother.

We're about to get into Part 3 of this book, which focuses on planning and execution. This next part is a product of the lessons I learned coming out of Covid-19, which produced my biggest setback. Our goal in these next few chapters is to create **realistic goals** that are backed by a **system**. They're the bread and butter of this process. So let's start buttering that bread. (Quick health tip: easy on the butter.)

Part 3: Planning and Execution

Chapter 9

Counting Alcohol Servings

What's in a "Drink"?

"Do not worry too much about your difficulties in mathematics—I can assure you that mine are still greater."
Albert Einstein

J ust as I was finishing my bachelor's degree in 2005, a casual conversation with a classmate revived an old dream. He mentioned that he was taking a gap year, bypassing the job market to globe-trot for a while.

On the podium of great ideas, I felt this was right up there with fire and free markets. I wanted in. But to afford it, I'd need student loans. So I channeled my inner Van Wilder and hiked down to the study abroad office. One application and two reference letters later, I was off to France.

Thirty-six hours. That's how long it took me to confirm two American stereotypes: general ignorance and math handicaps.

My first humble pie was served at a French produce market. I was sure a fruit salesman was ripping me off when the two units of apples he sold me looked nothing like two pounds. I unleashed my pidgin French under a furrowed brow, asking his opinion on what I should do with 14 apples and insisting this was the farthest thing from *bon marché*.

It took five Paris minutes for two things to settle in: the pounds-to-ki-los conversion and my freshly minted status as an American idiot abroad.

Shake it off, I told myself. There's only one way to recover from produce market mishaps: eat an apple, drop off the other 13, and find a watering hole.

I settled into an open-air café in Montpellier's Place de la Comédie, celebrating two birthdays before getting a drink menu. One glance, and a question emerged: *What the hell is a centiliter? Or 25 or 50 of them, for that matter?*

Having recently busted my budget on apples, I went with the cheaper option, feeling sure that 25 centiliters must be a 12-ounce draft. My server showed up, pushed his ear into my accent, and confirmed my order. "Okay, une demi", he said. I would've asked what a "demi" was, but feared adding to my reputation on transactions. So I just went with it.

When garçon sauntered back and dropped off a miniature beer, I was beside myself. Did he think I was a German ordering a Kronenbourg for my toddler? Another 5-minute reflection opened me up to the truth: 50 centiliters is a French *pinte*—and *demi* means half.

If you've ever been served 8 ounces of beer on a hot day, you know it's like being handed one square of single-ply toilet paper. Three gulps, that's what I got for my trouble. Later on, the humor came full circle. Turns out the metric system was invented in France in the 1790s and the last major holdout was, and remains, the United States.

Through embarrassment a lesson is learned: conversions and math make life hard. But to be aware of how much alcohol we're consum-ing—and mitigate risks—**we need to be able to calculate servings.** In the U.S., we're forced to do it with an archaic English system that doesn't use powers of ten. (That alone calls for three *demis*.) Sounds hard, but it'll become automatic with some basic definitions and a little practice.

Before jumping into calculating servings, a disclaimer is in order: Some people find the details of alcohol servings overwhelming. As soon as they see a math formula, they're out.

If this is you, I want you to know that I respect it. Life gives you enough to handle without hurting your head with liquor ounces, ABVs, and standard servings. That's why the same **tracking sheet** we used in Exercise 4 has sheets that will do the math for you. You just plug in the details. Go to the **book's hub** to get the sheet if you haven't already. (If you'd rather do it on your own, don't worry—I'll explain the whole process in a minute.)

If you choose to pass entirely on the math part, do your best to stick to common drinks that easily translate to a single serving—4 ounce glasses of wine, 12 ounce light beers, and so on. That way you can just count each "drink" as a serving.

But before you opt for the TLDR approach, let me issue a **second disclaimer**: "drinks" and "servings" are often not the same. In many cases, there's more than a single serving in a glass. There's only one way to know for sure: do the math. It really is the best way to know how much you're drinking and whether you're sticking to your goals.

At bare minimum, I hope you'll at least give it a try before deciding that calculating servings isn't for you.

How to Calculate Servings

The first step to measuring your alcohol intake is understanding the **standard serving**, or what's known as an "alcoholic drink equiva lent."[1] To figure out how many standard servings are in a drink, we need two pieces of information: the **alcohol by volume** of the drink (ABV) and the **ounces** in our glass.

The ABV of a drink determines how many ounces are in a serving. This is why ABV in drinking is kind of like calories in dieting—it tells you how much you can have before you exceed your goals. It'll be much harder to control your servings if you can't count them. Don't worry, I'll make it easy.

> Here's a simple formula for calculating the number of ounces in an alcohol serving:
>
> $$60 \div ABV = oz./serving$$

The formula should be read as "60, divided by the alcohol by volume, equals ounces per serving." In case anyone gets curious, I'll put the formula's full explanation in the chapter notes.[2] For now, we'll keep it simple.

Here's an example to illustrate:

A standard 5% ABV beer (Stella, Coors, Budweiser, etc.) would go like this:

$$60 \div 5\% \text{ ABV} = 12 \text{ oz./serving}$$

This shows why a 12-ounce Budweiser is exactly 1 serving. Actually, any 5% ABV drink will give us the same numbers.

As you can see, once you know your drink's ABV, all that's left is basic math you can do in your head or, at worst, on your phone. What's better is that it travels well. So long as you know the ABV, you can get where you're going. This is especially helpful when you come across ABVs that aren't as neat as our 5% beer example.

Let's look at another popular drink. Red wine ABVs range between 12% and 16% ABV. So, on the fringes, the ounces per serving can also vary:

$$60 \div 12\% \text{ ABV} = 5 \text{ oz./serving}$$
$$60 \div 16\% \text{ ABV} = 3.25 \text{ oz./serving}$$

It's not a canyon, but the difference adds up. A standard wine bottle is 750 ml, or about 26 ounces. At 12% ABV, the bottle will have just under 5 servings. At 16% ABV, it'll have 8.

If you drank half a bottle, the former classifies as moderate, while the latter crosses into heavy drinking. In fact, if you're an average female, drinking half of the boozier bottle in two hours is technically a binge. And the entire bottle in two hours is an extreme binge. As I've said before, binges happen fast.

The math on liquor—vodka, whiskey, etc.—is relatively easy since the ABVs typically fall on a multiple of ten. Run-of-the-mill vodkas, for example, are typically 40% ABV. Here's how the formula would go:

$$60 \div 40\% \text{ ABV} = 1.5 \text{ oz./serving}$$

This is why the standard serving for most liquors is 1.5 ounces. It's also why your local mixologist is taught that a "single" is 1.5 ounces and a "double" is 3 ounces.

That said, actual pours are notoriously bartender specific. An even-handed bartender (e.g., your local chain restaurant) will give you a 1.5-ounce serving. Your stone-fisted taverner, born reckless and feral, can easily bleed out 2 ounces (1.3 servings) and might bushwhack his way to 2.5 ounces (1.7 servings).

It might feel like we're splitting hairs on servings. But do the math and you'll see that it matters. In the previous example, you can have three cocktails of that first pour (1.5 oz.) and still be moderate. You can only have two of the 2-ounce pour. Enter the irony: What seems like the easiest drink type to calculate—liquor—is often the hardest to measure consistently because of the varying weight of the human hand.

If you're being careful about liquor servings at a bar, just whisper to your bartender that you'd like to keep it at a single serving per drink. They'll happily respect your wishes.

That's When It Hit Me...

When I started measuring servings accurately, it was mind-bending to learn how many I'd been consuming without realizing it.

You'll remember that I originally thought I was straddling the line between moderate and heavy drinking, estimating between 9 and 16 servings per week (3 to 4 per session, 3 or 4 times a week). The math of servings revealed that I was woefully underestimating things. It was actually *5 to 6* servings per session, catapulting me to *15 to 24* weekly servings.

There was no denying it: I was a high-risk, heavy drinker.

You might be wondering how I could've been so wrong for so long. It was basically bad information feeding a false perception. Before educating myself, I viewed a pint of IPA as "a beer" or any given cocktail as "a drink." Both, in my mind, were one serving of alcohol.

This was mostly convenient logic with a healthy dose of ignorance. But for better or worse, it was my view of servings. Turned out my mind was cranking out more lies than Newsmax.

I'll illustrate my ignorance with one of my favorite beers, Community's Mosaic IPA. It's tasty, it's local, and Susie loves it. High fives all around. The snag arrives when you discover the ABV, which sits at a towering 8.6%. The math looks like this:

$$60 \div 8.6\% \text{ ABV} = 7 \text{ oz./serving}$$

At Mavericks games, the end of the third quarter is a trigger for me...time to grab my third Mosaic.

One night, after a close loss, I deepened my depression by running the serving math during the Uber ride home. Turns out three Mosaic pints (48 ounces) is almost *7 servings* (48 oz. ÷ 7 oz./serving = 6.88 servings).

I clutched my pearls like a Tennessee Williams Southern belle. **Reality check:** I zoomed past moderation in the first quarter, and reached heavy drinking just after halftime. Math doesn't lie—this was a binge, pure and simple.

This story illustrates the importance of knowing how to turn ABV and ounces into servings. As I said, it's kinda like counting calories. It'll feel like a serious hassle the first few times. But it'll get easier with repetition. And like calorie counting, you'll learn how easy it is to fly past the stop sign.

The good news is that calculating servings puts you on a path to becoming more aware of how much you're drinking and how you're getting there. This is an invaluable skill for keeping yourself accountable and solidifying habits of moderation.

Chapter Summary

- Being able to **measure servings** is important for tracking them accurately and knowing where you stand with your goals.

- You need **2 pieces of information** to calculate how many servings are in front of you—**ounces** and **ABV**.

- Quick **formula** for calculating servings: $60 \div ABV = $ ounces per serving.

Exercise 5

Tracking Servings

BACKGROUND: Now that you know how to count servings, you can start tracking them more accurately. This exercise is critical for two reasons; First, it will help you understand exactly where you are today; second, it will give you a jumping-off point for creating goals later.

To track servings, you'll reflect on recent consumption habits *and* keep an ongoing count moving forward. You'll eventually have plenty of information to establish a baseline. The same sheet you used in the trigger exercise makes this much easier.

Neither your memory nor mine improves with alcohol. So when we reflect on our recent drinking patterns, let's admit we're gonna be off by a bit. It's most likely that we're underestimating the actual count. (Brains love to underestimate risks when something feels good.)

While this can make the reflection part seem fruitless, it actually makes it *more* important. We're not only going to estimate our servings—we're also going to learn how easy it is to misinterpret how much we drink. This will become clearer when we keep an ongoing log of our servings moving forward.

Step 1: Reflect on Recent Weeks

WHAT TO DO: Prime your memory first: go through your calendar and jot down any social events or notable outings, including where you were and for how long. Do this for the last month. If you're up for doing more, all the better. If you don't keep a calendar, tracking your whereabouts on navigation apps or ride share apps are good alternatives.

Once that's done, think about how much you drank at home. Try to remember the last few rounds of grocery shopping. What kind of alcohol did you bring home and how much? If you went to a liquor store or made any other alcohol purchases, write down when and what you bought.

Armed with this information, you can now key your servings into the "Last Month" tab in the sheet, or recording it wherever you prefer. Don't hurt your head too much with precision. Just try to remember where you drank, what you drank, and about how many ounces. (You can do easy Google searches to get ABVs.) The sheet will do the rest from there.

I tried to keep the sheet simple, so it only has one column per day. But feel free to modify it to suit your situation. For example, if you drank multiple times in a day or switched to a different drink, you can either add a column or change the header, maybe rekeying "Sunday" as "Saturday 2", for instance. Whatever works.

You'll notice that the sheet automatically calculates the total servings, daily average, Monday-through-Thursday servings ("school night" drinks), and Friday-through-Sunday servings. It will also give you a running monthly total and averages.

Once that's done, you can move on to Step 2.

Step 2: Ongoing Tracking of Servings

WHAT TO DO: Now comes the fun part: tracking what happens in real time. There's a second tab on the same sheet that covers the next four weeks ("Current Month"). Only this time, you'll have more confidence in the numbers since your fuzzy memory won't be part of the equation.

It's best to add drinks as soon as you have them so that nothing slips past. But I get it if don't want to explain why you're tinkering with a color-coded Google sheet when you're out. Just count those drinks when you get home or wait until the day after.

That said, if the servings start to add up and the count gets foggy, find a minute to record them, maybe during a bathroom run or something.

When I first counted servings, I did my normal routine: no cutting, no overthinking it. I figured that would give me an honest reflection of my drinking habits, which I felt was the entire point. But if you feel that time isn't your friend and you want to cut down right away, you should definitely get on with it. No need to put off habit change if you're ready.

Finally, don't forget to keep recording triggers on that tab of the sheet. You've already done that exercise, but more information in this area can't hurt. So add those triggers whenever possible.

Chapter 10

Creating Your Drinking Goals

Servings, Systems, and Accountability

"The more I drink, the less there is for the kids to drink."
Phoebe Buffay

I f you've already done Exercise 4 on triggers you know what sets off your alcohol loop. Exercise 5 made you aware of your servings in the last month. With that in hand, you're ready to make a moderation plan.

(Note: It's okay if you haven't done Exercises 4 and 5—start planning anyway. You can always adjust things later when you have better information.)

To maximize success, the planning stage has 2 steps: **setting goals** and **creating a system.** The second part is more involved than the first, but both are important. Here's the difference between the two:

- **Goals are the outcomes you hope to achieve.** They usually involve specific metrics or measures, like a cap on weekly servings or a certain number of dry days.

- **Systems are the habits and processes that help you achieve goals.** Rather than specific metrics, systems are based on intentional choices that build positive routines.

This distinction is important. Goals are great, but our culture is too fixated on metrics sometimes. Corporations, the IRS, men over the age of 12—they're all obsessed with measuring things. My daughter's kindergarten registration form had a gargantuan list of educational goals for the year. (I wonder where our anxieties come from?)

The problem is that **focusing on goals alone is myopic** since they don't give enough weight to **processes**. We can shore up the shortcomings of a goal-centric approach by paying more attention to the habits that help us achieve our goals: **our systems**.

This wisdom regarding the balance between goals and systems is invaluable. It has saved me numerous times from beating myself up about not finishing a project in a weekend or not meeting my weekly word count as a writer. (I'm failing at that *right now*.) All I can ask of myself is that I stay true to a system. Then I just let life happen around me and accept where things fall.

In the long run, similarly, our drinking-in-moderation success will be more determined by how good we are at creating a system that consistently helps us cut back on alcohol servings.

Here's what we're going to do in the planning stage:
- Step 1: Goal setting

  ○ Decide how many servings make sense.

  ○ Set achievable and measurable goals.

  ○ Create a plan to achieve those goals.

- Step 2: Creating a system

  ○ Limit exposure to triggers.

  ○ Make it hard to give in to cravings.

  ○ Introduce accountability.

Once all of this is done, we'll be ready to execute our plan.

Establishing a Baseline

When I started my planning stage, my basic goal was moderation. But I quickly realized that I didn't know exactly what "moderation" meant. So I dug deeper into the consumption categories, learning where one stopped and another started.

My first lesson was that you can be a social drinker *and* a heavy drinker at the same time. In fact, it's hard to drink frequently and *not* be a heavy drinker. I was also exposed to new terms like "excessive alcohol use" and "heavy episodic drinking."

It was a lot to take in. Let me spare you the digital rabbit hole by breaking down the drinking criteria from the CDC[1] and NIAAA[2]:

- Light drinking: 3 drinks per week or fewer.

- Moderate drinking: 4 to 7 drinks per week or 1 per day (biological women); 4 to 14 drinks per week or 2 per day (biological men).

- Heavy drinking: 8+ drinks per week (women); 15+ drinks per week (men).

- Binge: Bringing blood alcohol concentration (BAC) to 0.08% or higher in a 2-hour session. Typically 4+ drinks for women and 5+ drinks for men within 2 hours.[3]

- Extreme binge: 2 or more times the gender-specific binge thresholds (8+ drinks for women, 10+ for men).

I should note that many of these definitions add the tagline "on average." So "moderate," for example, is described as 4 to 7 drinks per week on average for women. This means you can have occasional excess and still call yourself a "moderate" drinker. However, if you binge once a month or more, you're classified as "heavy." It's also a reminder that each body is different and genetics matter.

Back to my planning process. When I started tracking servings, I still had the perception that I was mostly a moderate drinker who occasionally dipped a toe into heavy because of an isolated binge. I came to that conclusion through simple math: 3 to 4 sessions per week at a clip of 3 to 4 servings per session. This added up to 9 to 16 servings per week. Once a month, I'd go out and have 5 servings or more.

By the time I was done tracking servings, however, I realized my moderate-to-heavy perception was a farce. The pints I had been tracking as "a drink" became 2 servings. The 6-ounce glasses of wine became 1.5 servings. When simple math became accurate math, my 9 to 16 weekly servings ballooned to 20 or more.

At first, realizing that I was a heavy drinker was startling. But it came with a silver lining: I now had a good jumping-off point for **setting reasonable goals** *and* **more motivation** to achieve them.

Creating Alcohol Goals that Work

On the surface, a goal is simply an objective we want to achieve. But what really makes a goal enticing is that we believe there's a better life waiting for us on the other side, something we're lacking. When we fill this hole, we'll presumably be happier. But if we all have similar motives, why are some people successful in achieving their goals while others remain stagnant? Why do some people find the motivation to achieve while others flounder?

The problem, in many cases, is a lack of sincere reflection on where we are and what we need to do to improve. This results in goals that are unrealistic or—worse—beyond the effort we're willing to put in. Thankfully, *you're* going to avoid these pitfalls by considering a few things:

1. How much you currently drink.

2. The level of risk you're willing to accept.

3. What you're willing to sacrifice.

My goal setting was heavily influenced by the truth of my intake. In fact, it suddenly became clear why I felt the way I did. The lethargy made sense. The weight gain added up. The mental fog became crystal clear. What I needed to do now was face hard truths, especially about the risks I was taking.

I quickly decided that quintupling my chances of throat cancer or suffering from chronic fatigue wasn't worth it. But how many servings could I have to reap the benefits of alcohol while minimizing the risks? The answer to this question determined my goals.

Pre-Goal Setting: Current Levels, Risks, and Sacrifices

To set goals that are clear and achievable, I suggest following the SMART guidelines, making them **S**pecific, **M**easurable, **A**chievable, **R**elevant, and **T**ime bound. This means tabbing a specific number of servings per day and per week that are relevant to your situation and realistic.

Here are the numbers that are especially helpful:

- Your average number of **weekly drinks**.

- Your average number of **daily drinks**.

- Number of **dry days** per week.

- Number of **binges** per month.

Don't worry: The **tracking sheet** I provided you with automatically gives you daily/weekly averages. (If you still haven't snagged that sheet, you can get it at the **book's hub**.) If you're tracking another way, they're also easy to figure out by hand. With all of this in front of you, you can set specific goals that make sense.

It's okay if you didn't record your drinks. Just do an honest estimate of where you *typically* are in a week and go from there. Or if you know you're a heavy drinker and find the exercise deflating, just skip to creating reasonable goals.

Here's an example: If you're consuming an average of 20 servings a week with 2 dry days, a realistic goal could be 14 weekly servings and 3 dry days. A less realistic goal might be 5 weekly servings with 5 dry days. It's possible to have this kind of reversal. But you're more likely to get there over time rather than right away.

If you want to take out some guesswork, use the CDC and NIAAA guidelines for moderate drinking. Or you can come up with a more specific number that reflects your situation. Just make sure you cover the following **targets**:

- Total weekly servings.

- Maximum servings in a day.

- Number of dry days per week.

With that in mind, you'll have a good starting point.

To get an idea of how to set helpful goals, let's do some examples.

If a biological female found that she was drinking 12 to 14 weekly servings on average, she could decide to trim that down to 7 weekly servings to meet the moderation guidelines. There are multiple paths to achieve this goal:

- Set the number of daily servings to 1, with no dry days.

- Set the max number of daily servings at 2, with 3 dry days.

- Set the max number of daily servings at 3, with 4 dry days.

- Set the max number of daily servings at 4, with 5 dry days.

Alternatively, let's say there's a biological male who currently tracks himself at about 30 weekly servings. In this case, the guy prefers round numbers, accepts a little more risk, and wants to set his own standards. This leads to a personal goal of 20 weekly drinks. He might do one of the following:

- Set the number of daily servings to 3, with 1 dry day.

- Set the max number of daily servings at 4, with 2 dry days.

The guy in the second example could also opt for having 5 to 6 servings per day with 3 or 4 dry days. While this would keep him under his goal, it's important to remember that these high-volume sessions are potential binges that come with heavy risks. The occasional binge isn't detrimental, but weekly binges are. The best habitual practice is to keep the daily max at 4 for men and 3 for women.

When I first set my goals, I decided to follow the 14-servings-per-week standard. This seemed like a good starting point. I wanted to give myself some space for having more on social occasions, so I set a max of 4 servings a day and didn't commit to any dry days. I figured this was a flexible starting point that would get me down to moderation.

Technically, I was right. I also learned that *not* committing to dry days made it hard to stick to my weekly goals. This may not be true for everyone, but now I know that dry days are important for me. Michael Levy suggests a **max of four drinking days per week**, since "frequent drinking can escalate to daily drinking"[4] and bigger problems.

Having dry days will also teach you to do something other than drink and give you experience managing cravings. **Truth alert:** Habitual moderation leans on acquiring hobbies that don't involve alcohol. (We'll come back to this in Part 4 on maintenance.) Plus, the more dry days we have, the better off we'll be health-wise.

A popular alternative for setting limits is a **cap on alcohol calories** rather than servings. This might be a more attractive option if weight gain is one of your main reasons for moderating your drinking. The caveat is that it can be a little more complicated since calories vary across drink types and mixers. On average, however, you can expect somewhere between 100 and 140 calories per drink.

If you want to do this option, figure out about how many alcohol calories you drink using the information from the tracking exercise. You're doing the same thing, really, just with a focus on calories versus servings.

You don't have to obsess over your goals, especially at first. They'll grow and change with you as you go. I've even found there's seasonality to it. My drinking goals in summer, for example, are totally different than in winter. When calorie-counting pushes itself back into my life, I cut servings more or quit altogether. Then when vacations come around, I give myself some rope. It's an iterative process that you can adjust as needed. Just make sure the adjustments are usually toward less than more and stay true to your moderation goals.

At this point, you likely have an idea of how many weekly servings you want to shoot for, a max number of drinks per day, and how many dry days you'll work in. Write it all down or text it to yourself so you don't forget. You're going to use these numbers in the next exercise when you solidify your commitment.

The Letterman Lesson

David Letterman was motivated by a job. First, it was a job he wanted. Then it was a job he had. But the honor of hosting *The Late Show* was rife with challenges—competition, pressure, marital drama, and affairs all became obstacles. And behind it all was a drinking problem, steadily nurtured since his dad gave him sips of Cutty Sark at age 11. (Scotch. At *eleven*. Wow.)

In a recent interview, Letterman revealed what motivated him to change his relationship with alcohol. "I quit because I realized if I don't quit, there's a good chance I could screw something up and lose the job I'd wanted all my life. So that was the single, final motivator to stop."[5]

By his own account, Letterman's problem wasn't fit for moderation—quitting was the only answer. But his story reminds us of how important it is to have something to lose when we're trying to change. The dearer that something is to us, the more motivated we'll be.

Letterman was successful, at least in part, because the reality of losing his job made alcohol very ***un*attractive**. More importantly, he knew that viewers and the network would hold him ***accountable*** for his behavior by taking the job away. Simply put, he had something to lose and he knew it.

That same sense of accountability is something we need to create to keep ourselves honest.

Creating Accountability

If you did the why drill in Exercise 3 you already have something that motivates you. That's your version of Letterman's *Late Show*. But you should sprinkle some accountability on top so that exceeding your limits will be especially unattractive to you. A great way to do this is by mobilizing a **contract,** which will restate your **goals,** establish **consequences,** and designate an **accountability partner.**

***

Author's Note: I know contracts can feel overwhelming. To make it easier, I created a **fillable version** that you can download at **mindfuldrinkingbook.com.** Download the resources to check it out and see if it works for you.

***

Although all parts of a contract are important, the **consequences** and **accountability partner** sections are critical. Whatever consequences you create should be painful enough to motivate good behavior, but not so painful that you're tempted to cheat or lie.

I prefer consequences that start small and escalate. The first penalty should remind you of the commitment. The second should sting. The third and beyond should hurt enough to make you think, *Okay—I'm not doing that again!*

It's up to you to figure out good consequences for your situation. I find that money is an easy consequence, especially in the age of Zelle and Venmo. With a few presses of the finger, your accountability partner can demand that you pony up. This also makes the punishment quick, which helps connect the behavior with the outcome. Studies have shown that monetary punishments are effective for solidifying habits in the long run.[6]

If money makes the contract weird or poverty is an issue, opt for a chore. Wash your accountability partner's car, clean their bathroom, or rub their feet. The more repugnant the chore (or the feet), the better.

Keep in mind that pain isn't the only avenue. **Rewards** are also highly motivating and reinforce good behavior. You can use money here too, like a weekly deposit into a "treat yourself" account. Again, pick whatever motivates you in your situation.

For myself, I find it's best to have small rewards on a frequent basis: something sweet, an episode of a show, that kind of thing. Once you get to the end of a contract, give yourself a bigger reward. This is where massages, new ear buds, and "you" time come in. Use your imagination.

Whatever consequences you create will be more imposing if your accountability partner holds your feet to the fire. (Don't worry about the rewards, you'll remind yourself about those.)

For a variety of reasons, some people will opt to keep themselves accountable. This is the "on your honor" approach. It's certainly an option. The problem is that it's easy to let yourself off the hook, especially when the punishments are cranked up. A *good* accountability partner, on the other hand, won't let you wiggle out of your commitment.

All that said, some people will find that letting someone else into this process feels intrusive, so I want to mention a few other accountability options.

First, you can download one of the many apps dedicated to habit change and accountability. I personally use Stickk, which makes money a motivator while adding the twist of anti-charities—a cause, but one you loathe. They're usually political: anti-abortion/pro-choice, political parties, that kind of thing.

I won't divulge my anti-charity since I already get enough hate mail from my HOA. Let's just say I'm highly motivated *against* donating to a political party that has completely lost its mind. (See, that could go either way.) Plus, as long as you stick to your goals, it's free. You can also explore options like Beeminder, Forfeit, and Habitica, among others.

There are also apps exclusively geared towards cutting alcohol, such as Sunnyside, Reframe, and Try Dry. They all function similarly but have distinct features.

Sunnyside, for example, asks your reasons for cutting back, your typical servings, your age, your gender, and more. It will then use that information to develop a plan for you. The Sunnyside team says they use "3 science-backed pillars of behavioral psychology" to help millions cut back. I've found it helpful, especially for tracking drinks. But it lacks the teeth that come with true accountability.

Try Dry has the fewest features of the three. But it's also the only entirely free option. You get what you pay for—or, in this case, what you don't pay for.

Naturally, all apps come with a downside—they *feel* private, but they're collecting your information. If that's something that irks you, you might just keep it old school with the tracking sheet that I created for you. (At this point, "old school" means Google docs. We've come so far.)

As I type, I can sense that formalizing moderation habits with a contract might seem like overkill. But nothing is overkill if it *works*. Our ultimate goal, as I see it, is to improve ourselves. Let's use anything that gets us there. All the better if it's free.

I push contracts because they have been effective for me. Today, I use them to hold myself accountable to all kinds of habits: waking up early, exercising, meeting daily writing goals, and anything else I'm struggling with. Apps like Stickk give me an extra tech nudge. As usual, **there's a bonus**: We're learning how to use tools that will help us trim our alcohol intake *and* improve in other parts of our lives. The wins keep coming.

Chapter Summary

- The planning stage has **2 steps**—setting goals and creating a system.

- **Goals** are the outcomes you hope to achieve, while a **system** is the habits/process you'll use to achieve those goals.

- To establish a **baseline** for your goals, consider 3 things: how much you currently drink, how much risk you want to accept, and what you're willing to sacrifice.

- Your goals should cover **3 specific targets**—total weekly servings, maximum daily servings, and number of dry days per week.

- A **contract** is a great way to commit to your goals, establish consequences, and create accountability. They work best when you have a good **accountability partner**.

Exercise 6

The Alcohol Contract

BACKGROUND: Contracts are everywhere. At this point, nothing is certain but death, taxes, and agreeing to terms and conditions. This modern development has made contracts feel perfunctory.

Still, contracts are great tools for harnessing the power of precommitment and accountability. This is why they're perfect for breaking old habits and building healthier ones. It's time to restore the contract to its full, legally nonbinding glory by creating your **alcohol contract**.

There are tons of approaches to creating a contract with yourself. A solid alcohol contract does the following:

- States the **motivating purpose** (the why) of the contract.

- Sets a **maximum number of weekly/daily** servings and the number of dry days.

- Sets **start** and **end dates**.

- States the **consequences** of noncompliance.

- States the **rewards** of compliance.

- Includes a plan to deal with **common triggers/cravings**.

- Designates an **accountability partner**.

- Sets a **check-in date**.

- Has **signature lines** for everyone involved.

Sounds like a lot, but it's not complicated. As I mentioned earlier, I have created an easy-to-use **alcohol contract** you can download at the **book's hub.** You'll notice this contract does everything stated above *and* has two additional sections, one for creating a good environment and another to plan for specific situations.

Alternatively, you can type up a simple contract of your own that gets the job done. Completely up to you.

If you're leery of commitments, an alcohol contract might feel like living under the Taliban. If that's you, try starting off with something short-term and simple. You might, for example, do a two-week contract that caps weekly servings and threatens to dole out a mild punishment. You could easily do something like that through Stickk or Forfeit. This will give you a soft entry into contracts. Then you can decide if it's something you're into.

WHAT TO DO: Commit to your goals by creating your **alcohol contract**. You can either write one yourself or fill in the **pre-made version** I created. Be sure to include all the key parts, especially the ones on goals and accountability.

Once your contract is set up, there's only one thing left to do: print and sign. Don't underestimate the importance of this step. It deepens your commitment by making it a binding, physical agreement. Post it somewhere visible to remind you. Then all you have to do is stick to your commitments.

Chapter 11

Setting Up Your Environment

Making Old Habits Hard

> *"The first step toward success is taken when you refuse to be a captive of the environment in which you first find yourself."*
>
> Mark Caine

When interviewed by Axios, Sean Parker, the founding president of Facebook, was brutally honest about the platform's early intentions.

"The thought process was all about, 'How do we consume as much of your time and conscious attention as possible?'" Parker said. He added that they wanted Facebook to "give you a little dopamine hit every once in a while."

It turns out that this is why they created likes and comments. Parker went on to say, "It's a social validation feedback loop, exactly the kind of thing that a hacker like myself would come up with, because you're exploiting a vulnerability in human psychology." He admitted that they were fully aware it was manipulative. But they did it anyway.[1]

What Facebook did, by Parker's own admission, was make their platform addictive. And they're not alone. The apps on your phone are intentionally designed to hoard your attention, which is why the average American checks their phone 144 times a day.[2] That's once every 10 minutes. (Are you feeling the itch?)

Just over half of Americans admit to being addicted to our devices, while 75% feel uneasy leaving their phone at home. And it's clear why—our entire digital world is structured to be habit-forming. Peter Mezyk said that an app's success "is often measured by the extent to which it introduces a new habit."[3] After all, as the saying goes, attention is currency.

What makes digital habits sticky is that the distance from craving to response is exceedingly short. All it takes is a 30-second grocery line and I'm on TikTok. That's the power of digital pull.

Thankfully, unless we're in Vegas alcohol doesn't live in our pockets. But it has a drug component that most products can only dream of, a chemistry that makes alcohol cravings especially powerful.

Fortunately, you can offset that power by **making it hard** to reach for a drink. This is where building a healthy environment comes in. If we can create an environment that puts distance between cravings and drinks, we'll be more likely to resist.

(Quick reminder: the alcohol loop goes like this: drinking trigger ⃠ alcohol craving ⃠ drink ⃠ alcohol rewards ⃠ alcohol risks.)

I learned *a lot* from the mindful eating community about setting up my environment for success. Dieting gurus have been working on that since William Banting published his "Letter on Corpulence" in 1864. In the 160 years since, they've discovered the keys to creating a healthy environment.

The most useful tips are **limiting the home supply** and **creating hurdles**. Both have the effect of making it hard to give into cravings, which gives you a few more precious minutes for fending them off. These modifications will become critical parts of the system that will support your goals.

Limiting the Home Supply

The environment most in need of change is where you spend most of your time: home. Almost all habitual drinkers consume at home, at least some of the time. As we get older and go out less, in fact, more of our drinking happens on our own couch.

Covid-19 only intensified our domestic drinking habits, as we happily embraced alcohol delivery services who brought bottles straight to our front door. Once they were delivered, we obsessively washed our hands just before sullying our livers.

At-home drinking has various faces. Sometimes we start when we're out, only to get home and do our best *Thelma and Louise* impression. (Let's just keep going!) Other times, we start at home and pile on more servings when we're out on the town. Most commonly, however, alcohol is part of an end of day routine that helps us shake our daily stressors.

Each and every one of these domestic drinking patterns were common at our house. Our weekly date night, for example, usually included dinner and an overpriced bottle of wine. We'd then saunter home and open another. Eventually, it became a perfunctory habit to go through an extra half-bottle on a weeknight, *four* servings total for each of us. It's a fun date night, but a groggy Wednesday.

A **couple of dynamics** make it easy to overdo it at home.

First, alcohol is **too easy to access**. It's 10 steps from my couch to the fridge, another 3 to the wine opener, and a high stretch to the glasses. (Might as well grab the Thin Mints while I'm there.) That's literally 45 seconds between a trigger and an open bottle. This is like having junk food at arm's reach when you're cutting calories—unless you're a paragon of self-control, you'll slip up eventually.

At home, there's **also no accountability**. In other words, our shame meter doesn't register because nobody is watching. If they happen to be *listening* on trash day, that's a different story. (Clang, clang, clangetty-clang.)

Outside of that, we're free from public judgment at home. This combination of ease and freedom makes home an easy place to overdrink. This is why it behooves us to limit what's within arm's reach.

Luckily, home is also the environment **we control the most**. If you live alone, what comes in and out is entirely within your power. If you don't live alone, most friends and partners will support you by making some changes.

The two main strategies for creating a successful home environment are controlling *what* you bring home and *how much*.

Mindful eaters focus is on inviting the right foods into the house and passing on the wrong ones: buy veggies, avoid sugar, etc. The same logic works for us. If red wine cravings are irresistible, you might either pass on it entirely or be extra stingy about what you stock in the rack.

When you're controlling how much alcohol comes in, there are **two rules of thumb** to follow: the "**tonight only rule**" and the "**3 servings rule**."

The **tonight only rule** says you should only buy as many servings as you plan to drink that day. For example, if your daily max is 2 servings, you should only bring 2 servings into the house. This puts a hard stop on your drinking due to inventory limits.

The **3 servings rule** is similar, but caps the servings per person instead of using the daily max. A mindful drinking home should keep *no more* than 3 servings per drinker on hand. This means two wine bottles is one too many for a wine-drinking couple. In a beer-drinking marriage, it's typically anything more than a six-pack.

Sticking to these limits usually means changing the way you buy alcohol, which is what happened in my case. On the beer front, I never buy large packs (12, 18, or 24) unless I'm hosting a party. And when I get six bottles, I'll often create a mixed-pack that lets me get different types. You can scratch multiple itches in one purchase this way.

Wine still finds its way into our shopping cart, but instead of two bottles, I've gotten used to buying one regular bottle and one demi bottle (the half-sized ones). This keeps both of us under 4 servings, which fends off any sneaky binges. I know—the half bottles are a rip-off. But it's cost versus health. I'll take that trade off any day of the week.

Luckily, capitalism won the Cold War and free markets have flourished. One result of that triumph is an alcohol industry with diverse packaging options, ranging from tiny to comically large. (I've always wondered who buys those giant champagne bottles.)

Here are some **shopping modifications** that will help you limit your home supply:

- Half bottles of wine instead of full bottles or liters.

- Mini bottles of liquor (~1 serving) or quarter pints (~2 servings) instead of fifths (~16 servings) or handles (~36 servings).

- Beer singles (12 oz) or tall cans (20 oz) instead of 6-packs, 12-packs, or cases of 24.

Of course, nothing is foolproof and there are some potential snags here. One possibility is that you live with a fellow drinker who happily parades huge bounties of alcohol into the house. They may even rave about their velvety Pinot perfectly pairing with dinner. I know this problem well. When I was ready to wrestle my demons, Susie was joyfully carousing with them. (No bottle of red pops louder than one you can't have.)

I honestly never found a fix for someone else's habits. We can't control other people. Instead, we must exercise restraint. A similar problem arises during social outings, which I'll discuss more in Chapter 13.

Another issue is that buying on a smaller scale might not be practical. Liquor drinkers will quickly point out that retail trappings make it inconvenient for them to buy small—one purchase inundates a home with 50 servings or more. The only fix would be to stack up mini bottles from the liquor store. This is neither convenient nor financially savvy.

People with wine fridges or wine collections have the same complaint. After all, what fun is a wine fridge without wine? Or a liquor cabinet without liquor?

It's worth considering whether these collections of alcohol—and the fixtures that cradle them—fit your life anymore.

Reality check: If you buy in bulk to save money, you're setting up your home environment for overdrinking. Is saving money *really* worth sacrificing your goals and personal improvement? Is it worth giving up on your why? Plus, if you stick to your moderation goals, the money you'll save on copays will more than compensate.

For a variety of reasons—from entertaining guests to having an alcohol-oriented hobby—you may opt for holding onto cabinets, fridges, and club memberships. If that's you, your next best option is to lean on other methods for keeping cravings at bay. A good way is to put hurdles between cravings and drinks.

Putting Hurdles Between You and Alcohol

If we can't (or won't) fully control what comes into the home, the next best thing is to make alcohol harder to get to. So rather than limiting our triggers, we can **put hurdles between cravings and responses**.

The anecdotal evidence out of the sobriety community says that a typical craving lasts 3 to 5 minutes.[4] Therefore, the more distance, time, or effort we can put between cravings and alcohol, the better. Keep that in mind as you ponder which barriers to put up.

One common hurdle to use at home is a lock-and-key system. This is as simple as buying a beverage cooler or cabinet with a built-in lock. Then just delegate the key-hiding to a partner or roommate. If you live alone, put the key somewhere difficult to get to, like a tall cabinet. Lucky enough to have a guest house? Stick it in there and put it up high. The more work it takes to get the key, the more time it'll take and the more likely you'll be to resist the craving.

One Facebook group user wrote that she likes to layer her hurdles. A vodka soda enthusiast, she keeps her liquor in a garage fridge (distance) that has a padlock (effort) *and* she keeps the key in a safe in the master bedroom closet (more distance + more effort).

She didn't stop there. On top of all that, only her husband knows the safe combination. You'd have to be Lara Croft to get shwasty on vodka at that point.

Another great idea came from Reddit, where a wine drinker discussed his answer to a wine club predicament. It inundated him with wine, which he drank daily in an effort to keep up. When moderation became an imperative, he realized that he'd never be able to resist the constant reappearance of new bottles.

What's a wino to do in such a situation? He enlisted his neighbor to be his wine storage. The guy hauled nine boxes of wine to the neighbor's house, leaving two simple instructions: have as much as you'd like *and* cut me off at three bottles a week. The guy admitted he could have insisted and gotten extra bottles. But asking for more would've been embarrassing, especially after being so adamant on the whole thing in the first place.

Remember: Shame isn't always bad. We can transform it into a useful tool to correct our behavior. We just don't want to lean on it too much, as it can induce negative feelings, deception, and even giving up.

Beer and white wine drinkers have the advantage of temperature, since both are consumed cold. Chill what you plan to drink and leave the rest at room temperature. Or, better yet, in a warm summer garage. The time it takes for the next Chardonnay to reach a drinkable temperature should be enough to rethink the idea. If you're willing to ruin your beer or wine with ice, this option might not be for you. (Not gonna lie, I've done it a time or two.)

When it comes to creating hurdles, let your imagination run wild. What I've given you are a few tried and true examples. But other options exist. Hang your bottle at the top of a sequoia or bury it 6-feet under. I don't care what fiery dragon you put in the way, so long as it puts distance between a craving and a drink.

Chapter Summary

- The best way to fend off alcohol cravings is to **make it hard** to give in, preferably by **creating an environment** that puts distance/time between cravings and drinks.

- The two most important changes to your environment are **limiting the home supply** and **creating hurdles**.

- Two good rules for limiting the home supply are the **tonight only rule** the **3 servings rule**.

- Common hurdles include a lock-and-key system, physical distance, or even keeping alcohol off-site.

Chapter 12

Practical Tips for Moderation

5 Suggestions for Success

"The dictionary is the only place where success comes before work."

Mark Twain

When executing your plan, you'll find it helpful to have some practical tips in your pocket. **Here are 5** that I have found to be particularly useful:

1. Start with water, food, or both.

2. Choose your drinks wisely.

3. Find non-alcoholic replacements.

4. Sip your drinks, gap your drinks, and let go of your drinks.

5. Avoid drinking alone.

Tip #1: Start with Water, Food, or Both

For various reasons, thirst is tricky. First, it's commonly mistaken with hunger. Other times, we think we're thirsty for one thing and what we really need is water.

At some point, most of us have felt that the answer to dry thirst is a cold beer. The irony here is that alcohol will make us thirst*ier* before it quenches anything. This is because it's a diuretic that causes a loss of body water via sweat and urine. The end result is that we feel thirsty all over again and reach for our next drink, thus continuing the cycle.

The obvious solution is to drink water *before* alcohol, which will neutralize thirst as a driver of alcohol servings. A good gulp of water won't just quench your thirst. It will also fill your stomach, which will help you drink slower and, by extension, drink less. Try asking your barkeep to slide over a pint of water before a pint of IPA.

The only thing worse than using alcohol to quench thirst is making it a meal replacement. Alcohol is quickly absorbed through the gastrointestinal (GI) tract. It passes through our intestinal lumen, across epithelial cells, through the interstitial space, and into our capillaries (see figure 12.1 below).[1]

All of the GI absorbs alcohol, but some parts are more absorbent than others. (Why am I picturing a Bounty commercial?) Our small intestine, just past the stomach, has far more surface area for absorption. One of our goals, then, is to keep alcohol *in* our stomach and *out* of the small intestine for as long as possible.

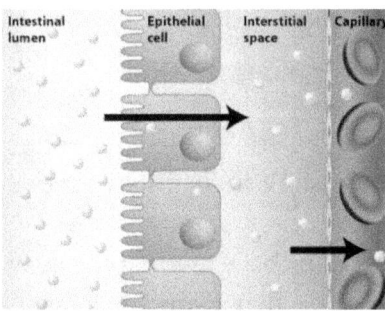

*Figure 12.1: Alcohol absorption
from intestinal lumen, to epithelial cells, to interstitial space, to
capillaries.*

We can think of food in our stomach like water passing through a Brita filter. When we pour water into the basin, the filter creates a slow drip into the pitcher. Without the filter, it would just pour right in.

Food in our stomach has a similar delaying function. It pushes back against alcohol, stifling the flow into our small intestine and slowing absorption. An empty stomach is like a sieve, allowing alcohol to move quickly into the small intestine for quicker absorption. This gets us drunker faster, the opposite of what we want.

You might be thinking, *Well, the bar has snacks—I'll just eat those. Problem solved.*

Not so fast. Bars intentionally pick snacks that are salty, which make you thirstier and a more enthusiastic drinker. It's a trick, don't fall for it.

One of my local bartenders offers candy as a welcome token. At first I thought, *Oh, that's kinda nice! What a swell guy.* Then the internet told me he was a sneaky drug pusher. Turns out that when we eat sugar it moves water out of our cells and into our blood. Our body does this to restore balance. The result? A sudden urge to drink fluids.[2] Which is then followed by a sudden urge to write a closed-fist Google review about the Candyman.

So what's a drinker to do? First, avoid processed snacks—in the Western world, they all have sugar or salt. Instead, eat nutrient-dense foods. Here's a list of **good foods to eat** before you partake in alcohol:

- Meat and healthy fats, including avocados, eggs, beef, and fish.

- Fruits and unsalted vegetables, including citrus, melon, sweet potatoes, leafy greens, and anything cruciferous. The more water content they have, the better.

- Whole grains and seeds, including whole-grain breads, oats, and quinoa.

The biggest benefit of whole grains and seeds is that they have fiber and will make you feel full. They also protect against liver damage, likely because of the antioxidants they contain.[3] You'll get the antioxidant benefits from most vegetables and fruits, especially if they're red or purple.

Your typical bar will brandish a menu full of thirst-inducing foods, like salty fries and spicy wings. Finding decent options here is like searching for good songs on a Bad Bunny album. It's a needle in a haystack, at best. The key is to find a **happy middle ground between satiating and thirst-inducing**.

If you order a burger, for example, pass on the seasoned fries and do a side salad. At the same time, think twice before ordering a salad alone—it might not fill up your stomach enough to have the delay effect on alcohol absorption. Throw some non-salty carbs in there for good measure, preferably from vegetables. Then try to sneak some water in between bites to leave you feeling full. You'll **drink slower**, which will help keep the **servings down**.

Tip #2: Choose Your Drinks Wisely

Because they have lower ABVs, some drinks have fewer alcohol servings than others. The upshot is that drink choice has a direct impact on managing servings. This is a good time to bring back our conversation on counting servings, which we learned in Chapter 9. Here's a quick refresher of the formula for counting servings:

$$60 \div ABV = \text{ounces per serving.}$$

Following this formula, we learned that it only takes 1.5 ounces of a 40% ABV vodka to get to a standard serving (60 ÷ 40% = 1.5 oz). This is why liquor is notoriously linked with overconsumption and high-risk drinking. But liquor drinkers aren't alone. High-ABV beers and fortified wines also make it easy to have more than 2 or 3 servings in a session.

Choosing our drinks wisely means seeking out lower ABV options to avoid this. That way, we can satisfy a craving without sacrificing our goals. **Remember:** The goal is to stay true to the limits we set in Chapter 10 and in our alcohol contract. It doesn't matter whether we get there through the front door or the back.

Fortunately, the market for low-ABV choices has grown exponentially. I've learned firsthand the difference these products can make for paring down servings. Simply put, it's possible to drink as many ounces as before *while still cutting your alcohol intake* just because of a lower ABV.

To get an idea how effective this can be, consider the following switches:

- A Bud Light drinker who switches to Bud Select 55 (just go with it) cuts the ABV of their beer from 5% to 2.4%. It's now 2 bottles (12 oz.) per serving instead of one.

- A Lagunitas drinker who switches from Maximus IPA to Daytime IPA trims the ABV from 9% to 4%, also doubling the amount they can drink for the same number of servings.

- A Grey Goose drinker who switches to Keel Vodka drops their ABV from 40% to 24%. Assuming a standard 1.5-ounce pour, they can now have 3 vodka sodas and stay under 2 servings.

- A white wine drinker who switches from a regular Pinot Grigio to Yellowtail's Bright Pinot Grigio goes from 12% ABV to 8%. It's now three 5-ounce glasses for 2 servings instead of two 5-ounce glasses.

Buying low-ABV alternatives is also a way of limiting our home supply. I mentioned before that we can buy smaller bottles to limit the servings at home. Low-alcohol drinks have a similar benefit, only instead of a smaller bottle what's inside is less potent. All these tactics fall under the same umbrella of creating an environment that leans into our goals.

One last thing: Shots, by definition, are not to be enjoyed slowly. They're the injections of the drinking world and are anathema to moderation. This is as close to a line in the cement as we'll find. I won't say no more shots *ever*. But if you come across an enticing Jell-O concoction, it's best to stop at *one,* and don't pour more alcohol on top.

Here's why: A shot and a beer will instantly spike your BAC and kill moderation. If you're a smaller female, the shot might do it all by itself. If you're gonna throw one back, chase it with something non-alcoholic.

Speaking of non-alcoholic drinks...

Tip #3: Find Non-Alcoholic Replacements

When lowering the ABV of our drinks isn't good enough, we can take drink choice to the extreme by going fully non-alcoholic (NA). This means replacing alcohol entirely with NA beverages that give us the "feel" of a drink without the alcohol. I call these replacements **rodeo clowns** since they distract us from our bullish insistence on chasing alcohol.

Here are some examples of what I'm talking about:

- **Non-alcoholic beers**, such as Heineken 0.0, Guinness 0.0, Coors Edge, and anything from breweries like Athletic Brewing Company.

- **Non-alcoholic (dealcoholized) wines**, such as Giesen, Surely, and Noughty.

- **Wine replacements,** such as Proxies, Non, and Spark.

- **Non-alcoholic spirits**, such as Ritual, Monday, Kentucky 74, and Lyre's.

- **Aperitifs** and **"ready-to-drink" mocktails**, such as Hiyo, Curious Elixirs, and De Soi.

Despite the plethora of NA options, this world remains a mystery to many drinkers. Some people are unaware how many of these products are out there and how far they've come. Others rank them just behind vegan "meat" on the imposter list, a collection of frauds that don't live up to the real thing.

I get where this skepticism comes from—being sold "wines," "beers," and "liquors" without alcohol feels like a deplorable scam. And a lot of NA products make dubious authenticity claims, backed only by paid reviews written in poor English.

Criticisms aside, NA products are the fastest-growing segment of the alcohol market. The common perception is that they're geared toward the sobriety community. And it's true that quitters use them to stay in the game. But cutters are just as likely to buy NA products. In fact, it's becoming normal to mix in NA drinks with alcoholic ones to trim servings, and they can be lifesavers during extended breaks like Dry January and Sober October.

Beer enthusiasts have a bit of an advantage here because they have higher-quality replacements. NA beers are often convincing replicas that taste and feel like the real thing. In contrast, NA wines have a much harder time accomplishing that. And NA spirits don't come close. This makes sense, given alcohol makes up 40-60% of a spirits' volume. It's hard to recreate the feel of something without half of the ingredients.

Even so, the ritual of drinking—like mixing a cocktail or popping open a bottle of wine—is often enough to scratch a craving itch, even if the drink itself isn't a perfect replica of the original. Plus, do you really want to recreate the taste of liquor? Probably not. That's why mixers exist in the first place.

Let me be clear: I think NA products are solid gold for habitual moderation. No single change to my environment has been more effective than putting rodeo clowns in my garage fridge. I believe in them so much that my subscription addiction now includes monthly shipments from Athletic Brewing and Better Rhodes.

All that aside, if you just can't bring yourself to drink the NA Kool-Aid, other options exist. Here are some other rodeo clowns that might help you to change your environment for the better:

- **CBD-, hemp-, and THC-infused drinks,** such as Cann, Green Canvas, Olala, and Sunstone.

- **Specialty sparkling waters**, such as Parch, Goldies, and Slide.

- **Hop waters**, such as HOP WTR and Daypack Seltzers.

- **Adaptogens** and **health-oriented elixirs**, such as Kin Euphorics, Aplos, and Jeng.

- **Teas**, including herbal teas and kombucha.

Some food for thought: research has shown that NA beer delivers a **similar dopamine spike** as the real thing.[4] Researchers think this is caused by the brain's anticipation of alcohol rewards, which it associates with the taste of alcoholic drinks (makes sense). **Translation:** The pleasure we get from drinking **isn't *solely* from alcohol's drug properties**—it's also about the **"feel" of drinking**.

When we recreate the sensations, we can still get a small piece of the buzz, even without the hooch.

Tip #4: Sipping, Gapping, and Letting Go

Western culture is fast and furious. At times, so is our drinking. It will help us to consume less if we make time our friend rather than our enemy. There are 3 keys to putting time on our side: sipping, gapping, and letting go.

Sipping is about enjoying the same drink for a longer time. This is something we should do in other parts of life—stop, take a beat, and appreciate things. **Gapping** is about putting time between drinks, usually by slipping a non-alcoholic drink between servings. Finally, **letting go** is about physically putting down a drink so it's not constantly finding its way to your mouth.

One way to master the art of sipping is to truly experience your drinks. It will take you a longer time to get to the bottom of your wine glass, for example, if you appreciate the qualities that a faraway vintner crafted into it.

It might sound silly or pedantic at first, but we usually just guzzle thoughtlessly, like our only concern is feeling alcohol's effects. Being more **mindful** and focusing on the **experience of drinking** helps a lot.

Full disclosure: This is harder than it sounds. It continues to be embarrassingly difficult for me, a person who has always been a fast drinker *and* eater, to pace myself.

When I worked on being more mindful of my rhythms, I realized that I walked and talked fast, too. It was as if I always needed to be in the next place talking to the next person. I also learned why my students often grimace in hopeless confusion during lectures—auctioneers on meth have a calmer pace. I guess I'm a good product of our harried society. So if I can slow it down, anybody can.

I've learned to use my smart watch to time just about anything: work sessions, breaks, workouts, and drinks are all governed by Garmin. When drinking, my current practice is to set a timer at 45 minutes and start it as soon as I take the first sip of my drink. My goal is to finish that drink as the countdown gets to zero.

It doesn't always work perfectly, but I try. If I finish early, I wait until the timer is done to start another. This pacing exercise has helped me master the art of sipping and enjoying my drinks.

When our sipping skills fail us, we can always sneak in a non-alcoholic gap drink to extend the time between servings. This tip is critical, seeing as the most universal trigger is an empty glass. Gapping is a way of strategically managing our response to this trigger.

Most people will find the most approachable, calorie-neutral habit is to order flat water with each drink. Then just make sure to finish it before starting another.

That said, there are other options, all of which are less boring. For example, several Facebook group members mentioned ordering Topo Chico before ringing up another cocktail. They found two things helpful: first, ordering it took time, which put more minutes between servings; second, the carbonation made them feel full, which made them drink their next alcoholic drink more slowly.

This is almost a foolproof way of avoiding excess. You can get the same effect with rodeo clowns like mocktails, NA beers, or soda. Your world, your choice. I would just caution that anything with sugar can have the unintended consequence of inducing thirst. The bigger point is that **sipping and gapping** are healthy pillars of moderation.

Finally, do your best Elsa impression and *let it go*! (I apologize for that joke. And for getting that song stuck in your head.) If we keep a drink in our hand, it's very easy to pick it right back up and take another sip.

I started doing the same thing with drinks that I do with my three-year-old daughter—put it down and let it be independent for a while. If you don't, it will never stop whining about how much it needs you and wants you to hold it. If you want to save yourself some pain in the future, give it space to grow up a bit. (You're right, this isn't about alcohol anymore.)

Tip #5: Avoid Drinking Alone

A lot of us have a tough time staying moderate in social settings, which I'll discuss in the next chapter. But don't discount the temptations of drinking alone. This is another context where we can *easily* overdo it.

We spoke earlier about the crucial role that accountability plays in keeping us honest. **The biggest problem with drinking solo is that accountability is nonexistent.** There are no social controls and no external judgments. Just you, the sheepish angel on your left shoulder, and the convincing devil on the right.

The absence of external judgment makes it much easier to give in to cravings and do things you wouldn't otherwise do. Need proof? Just run the montage of shameful acts you've witnessed in people's cars when they think nobody's watching. (They're windows, not drywall. We see you. And would it kill you to use a tissue?)

Alone time is also a common setting for triggers and cravings to arise. Consider, for example, our tendency to use "me time" to unwind and shed the stresses of daily life. Keep in mind that alcohol has convinced our subconscious that drinking is relaxing. This connection, as I've mentioned before, is powerful.

Once we embrace alcohol as a relaxant, unresolved stress becomes inextricably linked to cravings. Next thing you know, alone time after work becomes a convenient time to destress with a drink. This can easily turn into habitual daily drinking, which is a recipe for high-risk consumption. And if you live alone, there's little to no accountability to stop you.

You might remember that my own drinking story got especially complicated during graduate school. Part of the problem (on top of the stress and anxiety) was that I lived alone the entire time. My apartment became my fiefdom, a single-use space for everything—vegging out, studying, dissertation writing, and whatever else I had to do. Alcohol sounded great with most of it. And nobody was there to judge me.

If I'd had a roommate, things might have been much different. Maybe I would've found a modicum of shame in the recycle bin, or a hint of guilt in the "Stop'n Shop" liquor store receipts. But there was no reason to because the entire planet, as far as I could tell, was none the wiser.

You might be thinking, *Hey, I live alone and like to have a glass at the end of the day. Is that a problem?*

I hear you. And I'm not saying you absolutely can't. I'm just pointing out that you can torpedo your goals if you get into the habit of drinking alone—opportunities to drink are high while judgment is low. It's just not the best approach. If you're going to do it, make sure to set up the rest of your environment for success.

Chapter Summary

- Before drinking, start with food, water, or both to fill your stomach. This will help you **drink slower** and **slow alcohol absorption**.

- Choose your drinks wisely. Try going for low-ABV options to limit the number of servings in each drink.

- Find **non-alcoholic** (NA) alternatives that mimic the alcohol experience. These include NA beers, NA wines, NA spirits, and ready-to-drink mocktails.

- **Extend the time** spent with each drink to limit servings. Master the art of **sipping** and **gapping** to maximize the time between drinks.

- If slowing down is hard, try using a **timer**. If you finish early, sneak in a gap drink.

- If you can, **avoid drinking alone**. It's a low-accountability environment that can easily lead to overdoing it.

Chapter 13

Street Smarts

Being Moderately Social

"There are two kinds of people I don't trust: People who don't drink and people who collect stickers."

Chelsea Handler

M ost social drinkers find that the hardest part of this journey is being mindful when they're out on the town. It's easy to get caught up in good company and go with the crowd. This is especially problematic when the crowd drinks for distance, putting us under pressure to follow suit.

Young, untethered drinkers are especially prone to the excesses of social life. But they aren't the only ones. Drinkers who are past their prime, much like the young and free, often feel the influence of the herd on their choices. I started cutting in my late 30s and found that social gatherings were the hardest places to stay true to my goals, especially when moderation was a foreign language to my company.

So how do we cap our servings *and* keep being social butterflies? I've landed on **4 key rules** of mindful social drinking:

1. Know the setting

2. Make a plan

3. Own your reasons for being mindful (and share them)

4. Get your mind right

In this chapter, we're going to dig into each of these rules in detail. The overarching point is to help us control alcohol in a context where overdrinking is extremely common. So if you tend to drink wen you're out, pay close attention, since being moderately social will be critical to solidifying your mindful habits.

Rule #1: Know the Setting

Every social setting gives us new wrinkles—work parties are keenly different than best friend nights; lunch with the in-laws is a stark contrast to brunch with the girls; backyard BBQs are a world removed from swanky wine bars.

In each case, the people, place, and environment invite different behaviors. That being the case, we have to know the nuances of our setting, how it might trick us into overdrinking, and what we can control.

Anytime the gathering is at a home—whether ours or a friends—we gain some control. It's rare that a host will have a "NO BYOB" rule, and most will make sure you have cooler or fridge space for whatever you bring. This allows you to control what kinds of drinks you have at your fingertips, including type and strength. With this power, you can cushion the environment with low or no-alcohol options.

Admittedly, some settings make this harder to pull off. Imagine, for example, a summer pool party. It's hot, you sweat, you feel thirsty. This makes drinks—especially cold ones—go down a lot faster. Plus, you'll feel sexier in your banana hammock at 9 servings. Suddenly, drinking becomes a race. And you'll be damned if you don't win.

This sits in contrast to an air-conditioned dinner party, which has plenty of other things to amuse your mouth than Prosecco. If your gathering is a **fast-drinking environment**, think hard about your **drink choice** and, again, religiously **gap your servings** with NA drinks.

Being out at a bar or club is a little different. The minute you walk into a bar, you lose some control over your options. Fortunately—and finally—the service industry is now keenly aware that mindful drinking is a thing, and many are offering NA options and mocktails. In fact, and to the confusion of many drinkers, non-alcoholic bars are springing up everywhere.[1] I know it's a head scratcher, but it's possible that "social drinking" doesn't require alcohol.

There are plenty of straggler establishments that don't offer NA options. When you're at one of those the line of least resistance is starting with water and using your pacing skills from there. This will limit your intake.

The biggest enemy, however, is boredom, which creeps up after ordering your third ice water with lemon. When this feeling arises, get creative. Scour the web for more inspiring NA drinks to order at a bar and let the vine grow from there. Once you've done it a few times, you'll know how to order something more arousing than tap water.

Once you know the dynamics of your setting, including the nuances it'll throw at you, it'll make it much easier to make a plan for keeping things moderate.

Rule #2: Make a Plan

Remember that goals lean heavily on the systems we create for ourselves. Your alcohol contract (which is part of your system) gives you the opportunity to decide *in advance* how you'll keep your servings down. You might remember there's an extra contract section for social engagements. Now you know why I included that part in the contract: We need to tell ourselves *exactly* what we'll do to stay under our limit when we're out.

If a social event springs up by surprise, you can plan on the fly. You'll have experience, which will help. Just be sure to decide **what** you'll drink, **how long** you'll sip on each serving, and what to order between drinks *or* after you've had your limit. Be specific and give yourself different options in case one isn't available.

Some people opt for a monetary cap, which usually comes in the form of a cash-only policy—when Andrew Jackson is done, so are you.

When I tried this tactic, I realized it was ideal for nights out, happy hours, or watching a game. It also made me wish I had done it earlier in life. I have *way* too many memories of a grand old time being darkened by an eye-popping tab and the specter of not making rent. (Graduate school flashbacks...)

I found the online forum responses to the cash-only method were all over the place. Some people say it's an outdated method, since you can just Venmo a friend and have them buy drinks for you. Or, they say you'll find some other way to access money with your phone, like Google Pay or something similar.

All of this is true. But I think going cash-only is still a great way to put a fence between you and too many servings. First, it doesn't look great to say "Hey, can I Venmo you for another vodka soda?" The powerful shame factor comes into play.

Even if you can pay by some other method, cash-only limitations are still a solid way to remind yourself of your goals. It's kinda like cutting off spending when your checking account is dry. If you dip into credit cards, you're only hurting yourself in the long run. (But I'll admit the travel points are nice!)

Finally, there's a plan to think twice about. I've consistently read that some people make sure to drive themselves when they go out. This plan motivates moderation because they can't drink and drive. Plus, it gives them an excuse that they can express loudly and publicly. That way, they don't have to say, "I've been reading this stupid book about mindful drinking habits."

But if you walk this path, be careful. **Make sure that having to drive will *actually* keep you at a maximum of two servings or less.** And keep in mind that some states have zero tolerance policies for driving under the influence. Personally, I think it's too risky. The point here is to *avoid* risk, not invite more.

Rule #3: Own Your Reasons for Being Mindful

We may be out of high school, but peer pressure is still a thing. In the adult world it comes in the form of friendly drink offers or innocent questions about why we're not ordering our usual cocktail. It's not overt or aggressive pressure. But it's still pushing. And it can be heavier at work events, where we're extra sensitive to how others perceive us.

One study poignantly noted the source of peer pressure's power: It makes us feel different and isolated.[2]

In general, throughout life, we try hard not to feel that way. To avoid it, we often capitulate and go with the crowd. In fact, a study out of the UK revealed that **37% of adult drinkers** reported having more than they intended due to peer pressure, while **34% reported** accepting a drink offer because they didn't want to be rude.[3]

The best way to ward off pressure and isolation is to openly share your reasons for drinking mindfully. I've found that the more honest you are, the better your polite refusals will be received. This might feel awkward at first. But with repetition you'll be like a well-versed job candidate, locked and loaded for the "What are your weaknesses?" question. Only in this case, you'll be ready to fire off your reasons for trimming your servings.

When I started cutting back, I found myself furtively ordering NA beers or using the "I have to drive" excuse instead of being confident and open. How's that for a strange twist? Instead of feeling bad about *how much*, I became shy about *how little* I was drinking. It was as though being mindful was an admission of a character flaw.

To my surprise, when I started owning my reasons for cutting back, everything shifted. There were no PR messages to craft. There was nothing to hide behind the veil. I just started **sharing my why** with people. Here's a sampling of what I'd say:

- "Honestly, I've been feeling lethargic and sapped lately. I gotta cut down to get my energy back. But you do you."

- "Hangovers have come easy lately and hangover parenting sucks, so I'm trimming the drinks. But I'll hang out for a while."

- "This is the part where I have one too many and then I'm unproductive tomorrow. Can't do it. But I've been wanting to try this NA beer!"

- "Look at me—the wine calories are going straight to my waist. Not everybody can be naturally lean and sexy like you!" (Then pinch their cheeks and smack them on the ass.)

In a nutshell, **turn your why into a set of short responses**—then own them. This will make you more confident about your choices and how they're perceived by others. You might even find people agreeing with you and expressing that they want to cut back, too. (Fire up the Insta, you're an influencer!) This will make it easier for you to be social while also achieving your goals.

The only downside I've noticed is that your confidence can make some people suddenly feel guilty. You'll see it on their face when it happens, as if your mindful drinking exposes their problem drinking. Don't feel bad—it's about them, not you.

My best response has been to deepen my honesty and get real about how much I had once been drinking. This reveals you're coming from a place of personal improvement rather than judgment.

Rule #4: Get Your Mind Right

In *Taking Control of Your Drinking*, Michael Levy mentions the importance of **mindset.**

When you're drinking socially, mindset is about reminding yourself of your goals (and your why) beforehand. It's also about re-imagining what it means to bond with others. Our desire for camaraderie makes it easy to follow the crowd, including going drink for drink. Note that this isn't the same as peer pressure. It can be entirely subconscious and free of offers, questions, or pushing.

Mindset is one place where our drinking history is hard to overcome. When we were younger and carefree, we had zero problems combining social with sake bombs. But that same pattern can quickly become a liability as our life changes.

I moved to Dallas in 2016, completely untethered. To make connections, I attended Meetup events and other gatherings that always, without exception, included alcohol. Several years later, as you know, I have a wife and two girls. I'm just as happy, but I'm less free. Frankly, I'm in shackles. So I've had to reimagine what it means to go out and be social.

This mental shift can be a genuine struggle, especially in the midst of an alcohol-fueled gathering. It helps to focus on the "social" part of social drinking. We can be more engaged in our conversations, enabling us to make deeper connections. We can also divert our attention to any other activities that are in front of us. As Michael Levy himself wrote:

> There is much more to do than drink. You can meet new people, reconnect with old friends, or listen to music. Whether you are playing softball, swimming, dancing, or playing cards, you can keep the focus on controlling your drinking while getting your enjoyment from everything else going on around you.
> -Michael Levy, Taking Control of Your Drinking, Ch. 8

The part on activities echoes our first rule of being moderately social: **knowing the setting**. At some bars, the only thing to do is drink and chat. Alcohol is an unavoidable fixture, possibly even the main focus. Other places cater more to distractions. This shifts the attention away from alcohol, making it less important (or obvious) how little you're drinking. It's easier to keep your mind right in the second situation than the first.

In any case, try to focus on the other parts of the social environment—conversation, cornhole, cribbage, whatever. If you can do that, you'll have an easier time gapping your drinks or forgetting about them altogether. You might even discover that "fun" and "fucked up" aren't as closely connected as you once thought.

Chapter Summary

- Before going out, think about the social **setting**. Consider how the environment might lure you into excess and think about how to avoid overdrinking.

- **Make a plan** before going to social events. A good plan will cover what you'll drink, the timing of each drink, and any gap drinks you'll order in between.

- Openly **express** that you're trying to drink mindfully and **own your reasons**. Being transparent will make it less awkward and possibly gain you support.

- **Mindset** is critical. Before going out, remind yourself what your goals are and why you're trying to be healthier.

Part 4: Maintaining Mindful Habits

Chapter 14

Supporting Your Mindful Habits

New Identity, New Activities, Better You

"Life isn't about finding yourself. Life is about creating yourself."

George Bernard Shaw

In the maintenance stage, you're going to learn how to make your new habits stick, hopefully for good.

Most people skip this part, missing a golden opportunity to support healthier habits with a renewed sense of *who they are*, rather than just changing *what they do*. That's why our first step in the maintenance stage is to start truly *believing* that we're a different person—then acting like it.

Naturally, if you're reading this book, **you identify as a drinker**. Drinkers drink. Nurses cure. Doctors bill the insurance. You identify with what you do. You also identify with likeminded people. Non-drinkers are "them"; drinkers are "us." It's not just about a personal attachment to alcohol, but also how you perceive yourself.

Each drinker's life, to some extent, revolves around alcohol. That's why maintenance is also about finding new ways to embrace life, to find joy and calm in sobriety. So, on top of the identity shift, you're also going to explore non-drinking activities to fill the void left by alcohol. If you can do both things—think *and* act differently—you're more likely to solidify mindful drinking habits.

Maintenance is also a good time address the "F" word—failure. We've all been there, some of us often. I can't count how many times the "I'm gonna get a six-pack" fitness pledge ended with a shrug, acceptance of stomach fat, and a trip to Total Wine for, you guessed it, a 6-pack. (Mission accomplished.) In the end, we begrudgingly accept our foibles as part of our nature.

But as we kick off the maintenance stage, I want you to dump "failure" from your vocabulary. I want you to embrace your foibles. This alcohol journey isn't *really* about failing or succeeding—it's about finding which path is right for you. It's not a light switch, but a dimmer. Put another way, the **point of maintenance is to support habits of mindfulness**, not to spotlight flaws or resent personal limitations. Let's leave that to the beauty industry.

So even if you've failed before, find comfort in the idea that failure is *literally* not an option here. You might fall back on old behaviors, sure. But that's just a signal to rethink the whole thing and start over.

All that said, your purpose here is to stick to the new habits you've been working on. There will be slips and setbacks, which I'll discuss more in Chapter 15. But if you've come this far, I think you're up to the task. To quote my daughter's kindergarten teacher, you *can* do hard things—including mindful drinking for the long haul.

You can increase your odds of long-term moderation by **aligning your actions with your identity**. To kick off the maintenance stage, let's do just that.

Embracing a New Identity

In *Atomic Habits*, James Clear says there are three layers of behavioral change: outcomes, processes, and identity.[1]

The moment you put limits on your alcohol intake and backed it up with a system, you knocked out the outcome and process parts. Now it's time to cement these new habits by **tweaking your *identity*** to match your behaviors. New habits that are inconsistent with *who* you are (or who you believe yourself to be) won't last. That's why an update to your identity is critical for maintaining mindful habits.

I know, this sounds like something from *The Matrix*, an abstract notion that doesn't apply to real life. But it's actually practical and important. You have courageously set out to transform your relationship with alcohol. If you continue to see yourself as a "drinker", however, the beliefs that sat beneath your old habits remain. If these beliefs persist, past behaviors will likely sneak back in. As James Clear put it:

> The ultimate form of intrinsic motivation is when a habit becomes part of your identity. It's one thing to say I'm the type of person who *wants* this. It's something very different to say I'm the type of person who *is* this.
>
> – James Clear, *Atomic Habits*, Ch. 2

To tweak your identity, you're going to use two readily available tools: **words** and the **internet**.

When I say "words," what I really mean is the language of self-talk. This includes your inner monologue and the things you say to yourself out loud. You'll recognize your inner monologue as the voice in your head, which is probably your loudest critic. (Mine gleefully reminds me that an imposter, unproductive, and a weak parent. Cheers to inner monologues!)

Thankfully, you can **shift your language** in your favor. Here are some examples of self-talk that tie new habits to identity:

- A smoker goes from saying "I'm trying to quit" to saying "I'm *not* a smoker."

- A dieter goes from saying "I want to lose weight" to saying "I'm a healthy eater."

- A Canadian goes from saying "I want to own more guns" to

saying "I'm an American."

In each example, the shift in language is intended to square *who* you are with what you say you *want*. Drinkers have two alternatives to the phrase "I want to drink less." The first is to say, **"I *am* a mindful drinker."** The second is to say, **"I am *not* a heavy drinker."** In the first statement, we're embracing our new identity. In the second, we're rejecting an old one.

Both things are powerful. And in either case, you can make your own variation.

You might say that you're a damp drinker, a careful drinker, or a light drinker. Or perhaps that you're *not* an over-drinker, *not* a high-risk drinker, or *not* a binger.

First, focus on saying it internally. Then, move on to oral self-talk, saying it out loud to yourself. When you're used to that, start saying it to other people. The more genuine it feels, the better.

In essence, we're rewiring our brain to replace unhelpful beliefs with supportive ones. This is called **cognitive restructuring**.[2] If we're successful, our identity changes to reinforce our mindful drinking habits, making it much more likely we'll stick to them.

This *is not* just a random exercise to fill space. Clinical research has indicated that linking habits to identity supports behavioral change.[3] There's also a bonus: You can do this in other parts of life where you're hoping to improve. These lessons travel well.

Once I embraced my new identity through self-talk, I started expressing it to others. Then, something uplifting happened: Friends and family started making things easier for me.

On a recent trip with my close friends—gatherings that are notorious for alcohol-laced misadventures—the host picked up some NA beers and stocked them just for me. He knew I was focusing on being better, understood why, and wanted to help me stay true to the new me.

My sister-in-law did the same thing at a recent family gathering. Then Susie planned a yoga date for us, a sharp turn from our usual dinner and wine. And it all grew from being open about my journey.

More importantly, it made me appreciate the people I loved.

Golden rule for personal improvement: For added motivation, share your self-improvement goals with the people you love. What we tell ourselves is important; what we say to others makes it *real*.

The support of others is a nice segue into the next step of identity change: **connecting with like-minded people.**

There's an entire body of research on the role social identity plays in human behavior. So many things, from our politics to our sense of self-esteem, is caught up in group identity.[4] In other words, being part of a group can change how we perceive ourselves. This is why the sobriety community has long relied on support groups to increase accountability and prevent relapses.

We can apply these same principles for the purposes of mindful drinking. All we have to do is find our tribe. This is where the internet comes in.

When I Googled "mindful drinking groups" I came across a host of articles, sites, and social media groups that reflected my new habits. Everything started rolling from there, eventually leading to more nuanced searches, such as "dry month groups", "mindful drinking social media groups", etc. Similar searches on Facebook, Reddit, and other social media outlets will deliver even more options.

This process led me to sites and groups such as:

- Club Soda

- Sunnyside

- Hello Sunday Morning

- The Mindful Drinking Co.

- Tempest

- Moderation Management

- R/Cutdowndrinking (Reddit)

- The Mindful Drinkers (Facebook)

There was much more out there, but those were the highlights. Exploring these groups is eye-opening. I was introduced to diverse communities with varying levels of engagement and endless stories of alcohol struggles.

I also learned that finding good groups is a trial-and-error process. For a variety of reasons, some groups didn't resonate with me at all. Others were inactive or otherwise defunct.

After enough exploring, I found a lot of energetic groups with members in similar situations. I graciously pulled away from the ones that weren't for me and kept engaging with the good ones. The few that stuck made the entire process worthwhile.

Exercise 7 will ask you to join a handful of groups, engage, and put yourself out there. Like me, you'll quickly learn which ones are worth holding on to and which ones aren't worth your time. All of this, mind you, is entirely optional. But don't underestimate the power of group identity to motivate you, provide support, and influence your behavior.

Finding Alternatives to Alcohol

As we peel back on drinking, one of our biggest challenges is figuring out how to replace the time. Until now, our social outlets, trips, and activities have often included alcohol. Living a damp lifestyle often means sacrificing a few of these pastimes. As I can fully attest, this leaves an empty space that's tough to fill.

To this day, Susie and I still have a "dinner and wine" reflex on date night. And that's after a few years of practice. That speaks to how hard it is to find alternatives to drinking, a process that requires creative thinking. While it can be hard, this is another crucial step for maintaining your new habits.

When the search for non-drinking activities feels like hiking uphill, remember the potential benefits lying just over the horizon. You're about to open a new world of experiences. They won't just help you avoid extra alcohol servings—they'll also give you a new sense of purpose and vigor.

Keep in mind that **nothing solidifies good habits like positive satisfaction.** Eventually, you'll rely less on self-control to maintain your habits because you'll have healthier, equally satisfying things to do.[5]

There are troves of good news here. First, we're moderating, not quitting. This means we don't have to give up all things connected to drinking. Second, it's a great opportunity to improve our lives—we can strategically manage triggers, reduce stress and anxiety, and be healthier. Finally, we can learn how to be social without alcohol in the mix.

In Exercise 4, you reflected on your main triggers. This is a good time to yank those back into the fray since they'll help you find smart ways to spend your time. The best thing you can do is **find activities that offset your triggers**. All the better if they help you improve your physical and mental fitness.

Let's take stress, for example. You might remember that I had an epiphany when I reflected on my triggers: the potency of parenting stress. When kids run wild, so do my cravings.

I eventually found that doing some cardio workouts earlier in the day helped, especially kickboxing. It was much easier to kick stress cravings by night when I kicked a heavy bag by day. This fits with the research on the positive role exercise plays in coping with stress and anxiety.

I'll admit that I first discovered this by chance—I didn't set out to do something that would help manage stress, just an activity to busy myself with. But over time, it became clear that I had stumbled onto a pillar of maintenance: **physical activity as a way of managing stress triggers**.

Most of us share common triggers. But how we deal with those triggers is more individualized. Maybe reducing stress in your world means journaling, knitting, or trimming bonsai trees. Or you deal with anxiety by cooking elaborate, healthy meals.

The activity itself is less important than the overarching point, which is to give yourself an outlet while managing triggers at the same time. All of this will help you control cravings and support mindful drinking habits in the long run.

Thankfully, everyone's favorite information tool—the internet—opens endless possibilities.

A simple Google search for "group classes for adults" will deliver scrolls of options. People are always looking to connect, and organizations are as hungry for members as they've ever been. You'll be welcomed with open arms to a new group of people who already share a common interest.

Wanna hike? There's a group for that. Film appreciation? There's a class for that. Christian swingers club? They meet at IHOP on Tuesday nights. (Like the motto says, "Come hungry, leave happy.") Use the resources at your fingertips, and you'll quickly be burdened with a glut of options.

Here's a list of 10 popular non-drinking activities:

1. Exercise, in any form—bike, walk, run, yoga, etc.

2. Reading, including solo and book clubs.

3. Regular meditation.

4. Volunteering for a local organization.

5. Learning a language.

6. Connecting with pets, including walking and training.

7. Cooking and healthy meal-prep.

8. Games and puzzles, like crosswords, sudoku, or board games.

9. Writing/journaling.

10. Money management, including budgeting and investing.

Notice that most of these activities can be solitary *or* social. You don't need conversation partners to learn a little Italian through Rosetta Stone. But you can find an Italian-language Meetup group easily. Dealer's choice—either do your own thing or be social.

In the early going, engaging in non-drinking activities might make you feel like Neil Armstrong walking on the moon, awkward and unsure. But once you take that first small step for man—one giant leap for vodka drinkers—it'll be a walk in the park.

Just remember that filling the alcohol void makes maintaining a damp lifestyle *way* easier. And when you get used to it, you can drag other drinkers along with you, quietly proselytizing them into your mindful world. Don't worry—they'll survive just like you did.

Chapter Summary

- **Maintenance** is about supporting mindful drinking habits in the long run.

- Aligning **identity** and **actions** is critical for solidifying healthier habits.

- **Self-talk** is an easy way to tweak your identity. This means shifting your language to create consistency between your identity and the new you.

- Connect with like-minded people to capitalize on the power of **social identity**. Social media **groups** are a simple way to find your tribe.

- Positive **satisfaction** is key to cementing new habits. **Non-drinking activities** can help you find joy *and* stay true to your goals.

Exercise 7

Solidifying the New You

BACKGROUND: This exercise is about adjusting your identity and lifestyle so they're consistent with mindful drinking habits. There are 3-parts to this one. And I know what you're thinking—too much homework, right? But this one is especially important for keeping to your habits and solidifying the new you.

Here's how it'll go: Part 1 will focus on self-talk; Part 2 on finding your tribe; and Part 3 on alternate activities. As always, the **free workbook** makes this easier by giving you a structured worksheet to use. It's not too late to snag it at the **book's hub**.

Part 1: Identity and Self-talk

Self-talk can feel awkward. But saying things to yourself, especially out loud, is a proven way to support self-improvement goals. The reason it's so effective is because self-talk can change your mindset and transform how you see yourself.

WHAT TO DO: First, pick 3 supportive phrases you'll use for self-talk purposes. You can either use one of the following, modify them, or craft your own:

- I am a mindful drinker who's focused on being healthy.

- I am a careful drinker who manages the risks of alcohol.

- I am a light drinker who's going to stick to my goals this week.

- I'm NOT a heavy drinker who overdoes it.

- I'm NOT a high-risk drinker who binges.

- I'm NOT a careless drinker who drinks mindlessly.

Once you've picked 3, plan a time and place to say these phrases out loud to yourself while looking in a mirror. (If there's no mirror around, use your phone camera.)

Most coaches suggest mornings are the best time for supportive self-talk. But drinkers might consider their drinking patterns when choosing a time and place. If you tend to hit happy hour after work, then maybe 3 PM in your office is an ideal time. The person who drinks at home after the kids go to bed may find 8 PM in the bathroom is best. I suggest doing both—morning and some other time that fits your typical patterns.

There are also alternate phrases you can use in specific situations. If you're headed to a social engagement, for example, you might use self-talk to remind yourself how much you're going to drink and why. You might say, "I'm stopping at 2 vodka sodas tonight, so I feel good tomorrow." Or maybe, "No more than 2 glasses of wine so I wake up for yoga."

Do whatever works for you. Just remember that self-talk is a powerful tool for getting your mind right.

(**Quick side note:** Avoid negative self-talk at all costs. Slips and setbacks can make us feel bad about ourselves and open the door for defeatist language. This has the opposite effect of what we want. Always keep it positive.)

Part 2: Find Your Tribe

WHAT TO DO: Search for social media groups, blogs, or other communities dedicated to mindful/moderate drinking. Use whatever sites or search engines you're used to. Just be sure to search on multiple sites to get as many good hits as possible.

Most people will start with Google before moving on to Facebook and Reddit, for example. Others will opt for video content on YouTube or TikTok. No path is better or worse, as long as it produces results.

On each site, use appropriate search terms to find outlets. The most common searches and hashtags might include the following:

- mindful drinking groups

- mindful drinking blogs

- moderate drinking groups

- mindful drinking social media groups

- alcohol dry month groups

- #mindfuldrinking

- #sobercurious

- #hangoverfree

- #drinkless

When you come across potential outlets, **scroll through the posts and content**. For blogs or channels, you're mostly just seeing if the content appeals to you. If it does, consider subscribing or joining the mailing list.

When it comes to social media groups, you're checking on 2 things: content and life. Does the content appeal to you or fit your situation? Is there recent life or activity in the group? Do posts produce conversations or do they die on an island?

Once you've searched and explored, there's **3 final things to do**:

1. Pick *at least* **2 social media groups** to join.

2. Pick *at least* **1 blog or channel** to follow.

3. **Engage** with your chosen groups.

The **workbook** gives you places to write down what you discover and also suggests some helpful search terms in case you run out of steam.

How you do the engagement part will depend on your comfort level. You can reply to a post, tell your story, or post a helpful article. You might even tell people about any awesome books you're reading right now. (Wink.)

You'll feel much more like a part of these communities if you put yourself out there and connect. Just keep in mind that social media groups are public, so be as mindful with your words as you are with your drinking. This is the case even if it's a "private" group.

Part 3: Alternate Activities

Having non-drinking hobbies is probably the most important part of maintaining moderation. As you think of things to do, err on the side of simplicity and familiarity. I live in Dallas, so skiing probably isn't my best choice. It's expensive, far, and has a steep learning curve. (And a steep mountain.) The best options are relatively cheap, close, and easy.

> **Pro tip:** When picking a new hobby, do the "racket and shoes" test: If you have to buy more than a racket and shoes to do it, think twice. If you push forward anyway, cover up the credit card trail. #stillmarried

Rekindling flames from your past is usually a good option, especially if you already have the stuff for it. Dust off an old set of golf clubs, wipe off the yoga mat, or recommit to a Rosetta Stone course. Having experience with something will soften the entry a bit.

Then again, maybe there's a reason you quit the first time. If that ends up being the case, at least you won't be in for $500 and can easily move on.

WHAT TO DO: Designate 1 or 2 non-drinking activities you'll take up to fill the void left by alcohol. Try picking things that fall under the 3 "C's": cardio, creativity, and culture. Here are some examples:

CARDIO	CREATIVITY	CULTURE
Walking/Running/Hiking	Gardening	Dancing
Boxing/Kickboxing	Painting/Drawing	Languages
Yoga	Photography	Cooking/Meal Prep
Cycling/Spin	Knitting/Crocheting	Sightseeing/Architecture
Swimming	Organizing/Editing Family Photos & Videos	Music Appreciation
Team Sports (softball, soccer, etc.)	Journaling/Writing	Film Appreciation
Weights/Resistance Training	Digital Art/Graphic Design	Art Appreciation
Golf (just go with it)	Interior Design/Decorating	Learning an Instrument

This list isn't exhaustive, but it's a good starting point.

After you pick your activities, commit to some days and times. You don't have to be overly specific. Saying something like "2-3 times per week in the evening" is good.

If you want to be more structured, designate exact times and days. If it's something that involves a class or club, the specific day and time might be picked for you. This can be a good thing—one less detail to think about. Writing down what you'll do and when will make it far more likely you'll follow through.

Starting a new hobby is a good time for the **micro habits** approach, which emphasizes small steps to set yourself up for success. So instead of signing up for 3 power vinyasa classes right away, just pick one easier class and put the mat in the car. This simple set-up will make it easier to go when the time comes. With repetition, a steady habit will grow from there.

Chapter 15

Be Ready for Slips and Setbacks

The Bumps in the Road

"Success is not final, failure is not fatal: it is the courage to continue that counts."

Winston Churchill

I mentioned in the interlude that I fell off my moderation path when Covid-19 blanketed my life. The break in daily routines on top of pandemic stresses threw off my habits and revived my strongest triggers. At the time, like most people during the pandemic,[1] I just went with it. I figured that whatever was happening needed to happen.

While my path to moderation is unique, my story is not isolated. Most avid drinkers who strive to cut back will find that the road has potholes. Some dips will last for a night while others will consume entire weekends or more.

These **slips and setbacks** are normal and should be expected. Remember that a **slip** is a small violation of your moderation plan—a night or a weekend gone awry. A **setback** is a situation where you have to reassess where you are because things have gone back to where they were before.

My experience and research suggest that slips are typically caused by special occasions or breaks in routine. Setbacks, on the other hand, typically come from adverse life events that cause spikes in stress, anxiety, or depression. Since you're likely to experience at least one of these situations at some point, I want to discuss slips and setbacks in good detail.

Recognizing Slips

As I write, I have about four years of mindful drinking under my belt. Each year has come with, on average, about six slips. In other words, once every other month or so, I go over my daily max enough to call it a violation of my moderation plan.

I've learned that the best way to react to this is to admit it, hold myself accountable, reflect, and move on. Notice that beating myself up isn't part of the equation. With alcohol around, any given night can get out of control. The last thing we want to do is kill ourselves over it or pretend that it defines us.

I've discovered that slips usually sneak in when my routines are disrupted—vacations, annual parties, house emergencies, and the like. When routines shift on me, I lose the rhythm of daily life that I lean on to make good choices.

Don't forget that **habits are neurological shortcuts,** things we do subconsciously without thinking. No routine means no shortcuts—my environment is different, I have less control, and accountability goes out the window. It's pretty much a death sentence for maintaining healthy habits.

I'll illustrate with a personal story...

Susie and I hit a Halloween rager every October. It features loose bottles, a keg, beer pong tournament, and an outdoor fire pit. We book the sitter early and keep her on late.

Now, this is a regular event that I see in the distance. But it's still a once-yearly occasion that's out of the norm. And it has caused multiple one-night binges over the years, the textbook definition of a slip. (Legal defense: Technically, *I* didn't binge. It was Bob Ross, Fred from *Scooby Doo*, and a stormtrooper.)

One year, the hangxiety was especially sharp. I felt wretched *and* was a short-tempered parent, which is unfair to my girls. A few days later, I reflected and realized why this particular social event induces overdrinking: I'm out of my daily routine, I drop my accountability, and the environment is ripe for heaping on alcohol servings.

I decided the next year that I would wrestle back some control by taking some NA beers, getting my mind right before the party, and making an agreement with myself about how much I'd have. I still hit the party every year, but it hasn't caused a slip since.

Occasional binges at sporadic parties are worthy of reflection. But what's more concerning is when they happen repeatedly, or when our drinking goes back to the way it was before. Those situations are more likely to turn into **setbacks.** When these arise it's time to take a beat, rethink things, and make a new plan.

Spotting Setbacks

A **setback** is when you have to **go back to a previous stage** of your mindful drinking journey. (Quick reminder: the stages are contemplation, planning, execution, and maintenance.)

Let's say, for example, that you're trying to **execute** a moderation plan but are repeatedly soaring past your limits. In that case, you'd be best served by going back to the **contemplation** stage, rediscovering your why, and reflecting on your triggers and cravings. That, by definition, would be a setback.

Another clear sign of a setback is the resurgence of frequent, potent cravings. When high-risk drinking ferrets its way back into your life, for whatever reason, your body's reaction is to want alcohol more and more. Cravings are your body's way of telling you this. And if your emotions are off kilter—like in my Covid-19 setback—it's exceedingly easy to give in.

I've learned that setbacks typically crop up when life is negatively disrupted—worry, anxiety, melancholy, etc. As you know, my personal drinking story includes a stint of self-medication due to grad school stress. You also know that my biggest setback arose due to the trials of the pandemic, a dragon I slayed with a sword forged out of empty bottles.

I'll set myself on fire before doing grad school again, and I'm confident Covid-35 won't be a thing. (It damn well better not be.) But these aren't the last challenges I'll see in life. Whatever the future brings will test how I respond to negative emotions, which, like everything else in the future, is uncertain.

This is one place where we should keep a watchful eye. It's especially true for those of us with a heavy drinking history—we can easily have a setback when enticed by stress, anxiety, depression, or despair. And if those emotions were strong triggers for us in the past, we need to be *extra* vigilant. Sometimes we paddle well enough to stay afloat; other times we flounder, and emotional cascades ensue. When these feelings produce spikes in drinking that last a while, we're probably in a setback.

While hard times are especially dangerous, good times come with their own risks. Setbacks can arise anytime we increase our intake, something I do every time I go on vacation—beer on the departing flight, wine on the return leg, and however many in between. (Can't let those Southwest drink coupons to go waste!) The "beachier" the vacation, the more limes I squeeze into bottles. Eventually, the only thing darker than my tan is my liver.

It's a good idea to give yourself some rope when going on vacation, *especially* if you're traveling with other drinkers or staying at an all-inclusive resort. (This book is about moderation, not bad financial choices.)

But keep a couple things in mind: First, avoiding binges should remain a high priority; Second, stringing together multiple drinking days will resuscitate alcohol's drug power. This is true while you're away *and* when you're back home. If you don't pick your mindful habits back up, that hall pass can turn into multiple weeks of high-risk consumption. The upshot is that **setbacks and sunblock often come in pairs**.

Your best response to a setback is a return to basic principles: redis-cover your why, set good goals, build a solid system, and reintroduce accountability.

My setback lasted quite a while—a few months, really. It had been long enough that I basically started from scratch. Ironically (and fortu-nately) it ended up being a good thing. Now I know what a setback feels like and I'm aware that a good system is enough to bring back mindful habits.

Setbacks are also an ideal time for taking an **extended break** from alcohol, which is a great way to hit the reset button. You may even consider planning an extended break after vacations or events with high drinking potential. (**Quick side note**: Extended breaks are an important part of a damp lifestyle. This is why I talk about them in detail in Chapter 16.)

Before moving on, I want to quickly discuss the dangers of self-blame. Whether your hiccup was a slip or a setback, don't spend too much time punishing yourself over it. Self-blame implies that negative outcomes are a result of character flaws beyond our control.[2] This can quickly take the wind out of your sails and devolve into a "fuck it" mentality, possibly even despair.

As I mentioned earlier, this is neither healthy nor helpful. You're human and alcohol is an addictive drug. Don't feel guilty that it got the best of you one night, or even for a while. Negative thoughts beget negative thoughts and, in serious cases, can lead to depression. Please, pretty please, don't do it. Instead, try reflecting on the behavior itself instead of viewing yourself as broken.

That said, it's important that you hold yourself accountable. But once that's done, adjust accordingly and move on.

Reviving the Cut-or-Quit Question

Your relationship with alcohol is a living thing that will grow and change over time. At some point, that relationship was complicated enough for you to actively cut back. With careful planning, you'll probably be successful. But the specter of high-risk drinking can resurface for *any* of us. In some cases, it's fair—and responsible—to bring back an old question: *Is moderation for me, or should I just quit?*

Here are a few conditions that merit an honest reconsideration of the cut-or-quit dilemma:

1. You find yourself in a **ricochet**, which is when your drinking has gotten worse than it originally was. For example, 20 weekly servings have somehow become 30.

2. You're **lying** about your drinking. One example is dodging consequences by lying to your accountability partner. Deception is never a good sign.

3. You're going to **extremes** to drink. If you're rummaging through drawers for an hour to find the wine fridge key, you're going to an extreme.

4. Your **cravings** are deep and repetitive. Research has found that strong, constant cravings might signal a genetic predisposition for alcoholism.[3]

5. You repeatedly **exceed** your daily and weekly maximum servings, even in the face of strong accountability.

6. The **work or mental weight** of moderation feels excessive or exhausting. Counting servings and constantly giving thought to alcohol intake isn't for everyone.

If you find yourself in one or more of these situations, it's possible that moderation isn't for you, at least not right now. That doesn't mean you have to slap a label on yourself for life—you're just not likely to achieve low-risk drinking in the short term. That being the case, finding a better version of yourself means leaving alcohol behind.

If you end up on the quit side of the cut-or-quit question, know that the quit lit is full of great books to help you on your journey. The sobriety community has tons of forums and support systems, for people of all stripes.

Simply put, the sober world is no longer dominated by AA's 12-step approach. (That's not a jab at AA—they've helped myriad drinkers deal with destructive problems. I'm just pointing out there's plenty to choose from.)

Most importantly, you're not alone and there's no shame in coming to this conclusion. Quite the opposite. As I mentioned in Chapter 14, **there is no failure here.** Your relationship with alcohol is a living thing that expands and contracts. Quitting is just another possible stage—perhaps the final stage—along the way.

Chapter Summary

- A **slip** is a small violation of your moderation plan. A one-night binge is a good example.

- A **setback** is a return to a previous stage of change. This typically means going back to old drinking patterns for multiple weeks.

- **Self-blame** implies that bad outcomes are caused by character flaws. Whether it's a slip or a setback, this is neither helpful nor healthy.

- If slips and setbacks are frequent, it might be wise to revive the **cut-or-quit** question. It's important to remember that mindful drinking isn't possible for everyone.

Exercise 8

Checking In

BACKGROUND: The book's last exercise is about checking in on how you're doing. It's never a bad time to check on goal progress, but a few stages are especially important: weekly, monthly, and halfway through a contract.

The weekly check-in is critical when you're starting out because ditching old habits (and building new ones) is an endeavor that demands consistent attention. As you get more comfortable with your new habits, you can probably peel back on check-ins and do them less frequently.

Of course, if you find the weekly repetition helpful, just keep doing what you're doing. In any case, you'll want to check in periodically to make sure you're staying true to your goals.

Don't beat yourself up if you're exceeding your limits. That's not the point and it's never helpful. The point is to see what's working, what isn't, and how to move forward.

If things are going well, consider pushing yourself a bit. Maybe you can cut even more. If it's not going so well, maybe pull back and make things less strict. You might give yourself 8 servings in a weekend instead of 4, for example, depending on what's going on. Just don't open the door for binges, which will invite risk and kill your goals.

WHAT TO DO: Check in with yourself and your accountability partner to see how you're doing on your key goals. These include max daily servings, max weekly servings, and number of dry days.

If you're using the **tracking sheet**, there's a "Goal Progress" tab that automatically calculates and color codes your numbers. All you have to do is key your goals into the "Serving Goals" section. It couldn't be easier. Be sure to **share that document with your accountability partner** so they can stay on top of you!

As always, you can also choose to do your own progress tracking. Whatever route you choose, make sure to cover some **key points** when checking in:

1. Are you meeting your daily and weekly **max serving goals**?

2. Are you sticking to the **number of dry days**?

3. If you are staying under your max servings, **what's working for you**?

4. If you're exceeding your max servings, what's the cause? Where did things go wrong and **what's not working**?

5. If any **adjustments** are needed, what are they? (More dry days, other changes to your environment, etc.)

6. Have you held yourself **accountable** with consequences? Have you **rewarded** yourself when you succeed?

If you're at the **end of a contract**, you can go a bit further:

- Were your **goals** realistic, too strict, or not strict enough?

- Were you **motivated** by the **consequences/rewards** you set up?

- Did your **accountability partner** play their role well?

- Reconnect with **your why**—is it still giving you the motivation you need?

- **Refresh and revise** the contract as you start a new one.

Look back at your tracking sheet with your accountability partner and compare it with your contract. I've included a check-in worksheet in the **free workbook** that covers all the important points.

This probably seems like a lot of work. But don't worry: This check-in process will become habitual and easy.

You should designate a check-in date in each contract, but feel free to do it as often as you want. Most importantly, make sure to be honest in your reflections and adjust when things aren't working.

Chapter 16

The Value of Extended Breaks

Are You Ready for A Dry Month?

"If January is the month of change, February is the month of lasting change."

Marc Parent

I was first exposed to extended alcohol breaks the same way most people are, namely through social media. I've long since forgotten who, but someone wrote a Sober October post about hitting the reset button on their drinking. The skeptic in me was instantly triggered. Why, I wondered, would any drinker take on such a foolhardy commitment? (That says something about where I was.)

But my doubt quickly turned to curiosity and, eventually, to genuine interest. Lots of people were doing it. Why not try it? Millions of people have had a similar experience, eventually seeing the virtues of extended breaks after being exposed to mindful culture.

The rising popularity of dry months has been monumental for mindful drinking. Like most other things, alcohol consumption has trends. So when social media feeds light up with messages about taking a break, people perceive a trend and buy in. The result has been a renewed focus on peeling away alcohol for large chunks of time. The movement is so potent that bar owners widely complain it's hurting their bottom line.[1] (Don't cry, they'll live.)

Dry January, the most popular of the dry month movements, first started in the UK in 2013 with 4,000 participants. Today, tens of millions of people hop on the New Year's bandwagon each year. (I'm willing to bet half of them have a drink by MLK day, but at least they tried.)

Today, we have copycat "dryathlon" movements spread across the calendar: March Forth, Mindful May, Dry June, Dry July, and Sober October are all trending hashtags when their time comes. The word is out. If you haven't done so already, it may be time for you to join the crowd.

In this chapter, we're going to see why a month off can be a shot in the arm for mindfulness. What are the most tangible benefits? How do you know when you're ready to make this commitment? The answers will give you an idea how to insert extended breaks into your relationship with alcohol.

The Benefits of Extended Breaks

While they might sound like momentary fad diets, extended breaks have real, long-term benefits.

11 Key Benefits of an Extended Alcohol Break:

1. Reset of your body's **chemical relationship** with alcohol.

2. Reduced **negative health outcomes** stemming from alcohol, such as inflammation and gut health.

3. **Liver recovery** and repair.

4. Re-establishing **healthy sleeping** patterns.

5. Improved **appearance**, including healthier skin and eyes.

6. Upticks in account balances because of **saving money**.

7. A trimmed waistline.

8. A **renewed focus** on the more important parts of life, like work and family.

9. More time for **healthier pursuits**, like reading and working out.

10. Personal lessons on how to live your daily life without alcohol.

11. Arriving at an honest, detached mindset about drinking.

The **physical benefits** of taking a vacation from alcohol are well-documented. For example, a cross-national study found that people who gave up alcohol for a month saw significant improvements in metabolic health, decreases in blood pressure, sharp reductions in insulin resistance, and drops in cancer-related growth factors. All of this happened with little to no changes in diet or exercise and none of these improvements were observed in the control group.[2]

It gets better: when researchers followed up with the participants six months later, the dry group had maintained a reduction in their alcohol intake. They had gone, on average, from "hazardous" drinking to "low-risk" drinking.

This echoed another Dry January study, which found that participants drank less frequently, dropping from 4 days per week to 3 days per week, on average. At the six month check-in, participants also reported getting drunk less often, down from an average of 3.5 times per month to 2 times per month.

Researchers attributed the long-term success to something they called "drink refusal self-efficacy."[3] Translation: people learned how to spend their time doing something other than drinking, which made it easier to abstain.

Thickening the argument for long pauses is that several of the benefits take time. Better skin and improved sleep, for example, take *at least* a week to surface. Others, like liver repair, take even longer.

Think about it—avid drinkers have typically been bruising their livers for years, possibly decades. Thinking we can fix that in a weekend is like doing morning sit-ups for an afternoon pool party. (Doesn't work, I tried.) This is one good reason, among many, for peppering extended breaks into your moderation plan.

A Launchpad for Healthier Habits

The lasting impact of extended breaks is why they're ideal for strengthening mindful habits.[4] A month is enough to tame our strongest cravings. Just as importantly, dry stints teach us how to be different people. In 30-ish days, you'll have no choice but to find other things to do, discover new places, and reevaluate your social life. It might be a bumpy ride at times. But the result will be a new level of empowerment. And that will likely happen even if you don't go the full month without a drink.

Another piece of good news is that extended breaks get easier with repetition. My first so-called "break" was a Sober October full of cravings, occasional glasses of wine, and an Oktoberfest outing. (Guess how that went...) A few years later, with multiple Dry Januarys and Dry Julys mixed in, I have a much easier time getting through unscathed. It's a learning process, like anything else.

One of the best parts is that the popularity of sober months has normalized the practice. No explanations required. No weird looks or comments. You can just say, "I'm doing Dry January." All you'll get is affirming nods and others wanting to jump on the wagon.

It's also easy to combine dry months with other health habits, such as new exercise programs or calorie goals. Honestly, it's *the* ideal time for toning up and losing the wine waist. Why? Because it's *really* hard to shed fat *and* drink at the same time, especially when you're north of 30.

Are You Ready for an Extended Break?

You're just getting started on your mindful journey, so I don't want to pressure you to take on an extended break before you're there. Feeling ready is an important starting point. If you're not prepared to commit, you might not finish the month and shame yourself for it.

That said, there are a couple of signs you're ready to embrace a month off. The first is **success**. If you're doing a good job of staying moderate, a dry month is a great way to crank things up a notch. It's kinda like starting a workout routine. You don't jump straight into an elite crossfit competition—you ease yourself in. Then, with time, you challenge yourself. The same idea fits here.

The second reason, oddly, is a **lack of success**. Let's say you're experiencing multiple slips in a short period of time. First, don't beat yourself up over it. Maybe you're just one of those people who needs an extended break to kick high-risk habits to the curb.

Studies have shown that long breaks are a great way to kick cravings and set yourself up for long-term success. So consider trying it if you're truly motivated to exorcise the craving demons. Just be sure to make a solid plan first.

There are some basic strategies that will help you take a monthslong sabbatical from the drinking world. A lot of what we talked about in Chapter 10, Chapter 11, and Chapter 12 is useful. Prep your environment, build your contract, and create accountability.

Perhaps most importantly, start thinking about how you'll spend your time. (Maybe your money, too, since you'll be saving some.) What will you do on date night? What will you order with dinner? Which new workout program will you take up? What kind of tea will you brew at night?

This is a new you with healthier interests. Be open, use your imagination, and figure out what they are. *That* is the key to making a dry month a smooth process.

Chapter 17

Looking Forward: The New You

"If you are enjoying your life, you'll feel much less desire to escape from it."

Frederick Rotgers

As I type, I'm starting a month-long extended break from alcohol. This comes after a weekend with best friends in the Pacific Northwest and a family vacation to the South Carolina coast. Eight days, lots of familiar faces, Oregon wine country, warm beach days, and old drinking reflexes.

The result? About 20 alcohol servings in a week—although I'll be honest that I wasn't religiously counting. I never got *drunk*. But I gave myself the freedom to roam into spaces I rarely go these days. And I did so knowingly, without self-flagellation or judgment. Now it's time to spring back, take a break, and hit the reset button all over again.

So here I am, revisiting this book's lessons and dusting off old tools. If you keep alcohol in your life, you'll probably do the same thing at some point. Living damp typically means there are ebbs and flows. You'll occasionally have to refocus, create new goals, loosen a little here, and tighten a little there.

This isn't necessarily bad. It's a normal consequence of keeping alcohol in our lives. The good news is, unless there's a dependence issue, resetting will get much easier with time and repetition.

This is a great time to recap our journey. Here's a quick look at where we've been:

- We contemplated our **why.** These are our deepest reasons for wanting to change how we drink. Our why became the fuel in our tank and a clear set of motivations.

- We learned about **habits and the alcohol loop**, including triggers, cravings, rewards, and risks. This included grappling with the allure of alcohol and how it can lead us into excess.

- We delved into our **personal triggers and consumption patterns.** This involved identifying the places, faces, and emotions that set off the alcohol loop as well as tracking our servings.

- We learned about alcohol's **benefits and risks.** Remember that the benefits are primarily social and relational while the risks are mostly health related.

- We created **alcohol goals and mobilized alcohol contracts** to make ourselves accountable.

- We **created a system** that maximized our chances for success. This included building a healthy environment that made it hard to overdrink.

- We embraced a **new identity** as mindful drinkers and adopted a lifestyle that's compatible with that identity.

- We learned about the importance of taking **extended breaks** and other new challenges.

You probably found some of the lessons more useful than others. Some might not have been useful to you at all. Moving forward, keep what's helpful at your fingertips. Then feel free to leave the rest behind.

That said, if you have multiple slips or a setback, consider revisiting everything with an open mind. The second time you read a book it's different from the first. Even the third time, you'll notice things you didn't before. This book is no different.

I put extra thought into making this a practical book. That's why I created exercises and asked you to put a little time into doing them. I believe in their utility and sincerely hope that they were beneficial. They're also malleable, so modify them to fit your needs. You might even find them useful for other parts of your life.

I use the same why drills from Exercise 3 to find motivation for a lot of things, not just capping my servings. I try to spot triggers for bad eating habits, like we did in Exercise 4. And at this point, I use contracts more than T-Mobile.

All of these exercises are taken from habit experts and clinicians. If you come back to this book for whatever reason, don't skip over the exercises because you've already been there. They're the meat on the bones.

All of that aside, I get that I'm no Nicholas Sparks and this book *might not* be worth a second roll in the hay. That's why I gladly offered the **workbook** and **tracking sheet** to my readers. Together, they're basically a curated package with all the important stuff—tools, exercises, and knowledge. That way, you can see the pearls without having to pry open the clam.

What Happens Now?

This has always been a choose-your-own-adventure journey. With a little guidance, you've picked the path that makes the most sense to you. That will continue to be the case as you move forward. I hope this is an empowering feeling, a stronger grip on a better life. You now have the tools and knowledge you need to make wise choices about your relationship with alcohol.

Remember: Today is heavily conditioned by what you did yesterday, and tomorrow by what you do today. This is what economists refer to as "path dependency." It serves as a reminder that **your past choices matter, collectively adding up to the current version of "you."** In other words, your life has its own butterfly effect.

In the drinker's world, our path requires **vigilance**. Vigilance of alcohol's role in our lives. But also vigilance of **where we are** on any given day and how alcohol fits in. We might even need to consider if it fits at all one day.

Here's the reality: There are many possible sequels to this book, myriad paths our journey can take. Maybe there's a hairpin left turn up ahead. Or perhaps it'll be a smooth downhill cruise. What I love is that we have the power and tools to guide us to the best avenue.

As we close things out, I'd like to discuss the typical paths forward. When I say "paths," I mean that most of us will end up in 1 of 5 possible places on the drinking front. I'll call them **damp, slippery, dry, sober,** and **problematic.** Before closing out the book, let's review each path so we know what to look for.

Path #1: Damp

What most defines the damp path is **successful moderation and maintaining habits of mindfulness.** These habits become almost automatic and are cemented into a person's life. Throughout this book, this is what we've been aiming for. It likely means the person has successfully taken on the identity of a mindful drinker and stays true to it.

While there's room for individual differences, damp drinkers typically **hold at moderate or light drinking levels.** This usually means one or two servings a night, on average.

Keep in mind that damp drinkers can have slips from time to time, possibly even a few binges a year. (Remember that a slip is a small, isolated fall from moderation. A random one-night binge, for example.)

Damp drinkers can give themselves some room on special occasions or vacations, but they're usually good at managing servings. The biggest danger is overconfidence, which can result in more slips than the damp drinker would prefer. If this happens, it can become a slippery slope that takes us to a different place.

Path #2: Slippery

The slippery path is when a person wants to live a damp, mindful lifestyle but with **repeated slips and occasional setbacks.** (Remember that a setback is when you have to fully reassess you're drinking because you're back where you started.) If you're repeatedly exceeding serving limits, binging too frequently, or feel like you're spinning your wheels, you're probably on the slippery path.

You can respond to this in multiple ways. The first is to **keep learning while retooling your environment.** Are there triggers you haven't exposed? Have you put enough distance between you and alcohol to help manage cravings? Is your social world too alcohol-centric? What are your alternate activities? Go back to the planning stage and see what you can change to induce better habits. Then try again.

Another response is to **wipe the slate clean by taking an extended break.** Then—and only after a *successful* break—make another moderation plan. Sometimes that's what it takes to peel away those cravings.

Slippery, as the word suggests, can signal that your grip on alcohol is tenuous. As such, **it can easily lead to the problematic path.** This might be the case if you're having frequent setbacks or ricochets.

Path #3: Problematic

The problematic path happens when **repeated attempts at moderation** (and even extended breaks) **don't end with healthier drinking habits.** In a nutshell, old patterns continually resurface. These include heavy drinking, high-risk behavior, blackouts, and possibly worse. The result is **repeated setbacks** and **possibly ricochets.** (Remember that a ricochet is when a drinking problem becomes worse than it originally was.)

In these cases, clinicians typically suggest full abstention. (AKA the sober path, which we'll discuss in a minute.) This is because the person likely has a genetic predisposition for severe alcohol use disorder.

Experts have some important wisdom for those on the problematic path.[1] First, **there is no shame in admitting that moderation didn't work for you.** In fact, this can be the most empowering moment in a drinker's journey and a signal to embrace a sober identity. This by itself could usher in a better life.

Second, **sobriety doesn't have to feel like eternal damnation.** It's common for people to find they can drink again after abstaining for a while. People change. They might mature out of their drinking problems after a sober stint, or they can adopt the "one day at a time method" seen in the AA approach. Nothing is forever. So don't let sobriety feel like a daunting weight on your shoulders.

If you find yourself experiencing repeated setbacks or ricochets, it may be time to seek professional help or support. Here are some outlets:

- SMART Recovery

- LifeRing Secular Recovery

- Secular Organizations for Sobriety

- Women for Sobriety

- Alcoholics Anonymous

There are also wonderful books in the quit lit to help you on your journey. The answers you find *are not* admissions of failure. The help you get *does not* mean you're broken. The new life you embrace *is not* a lesser one. It's just a different path.

Path #4: Dry

The dry path is when a person is **mostly sober,** but leaves the door open for **occasional drinking.** In plain terms, alcohol is no longer a routine part of their life. It just pops up on holidays, weddings, vacations, and the like.

There are multiple ways to arrive on the dry path. For some, things are too slippery or problematic for comfort. Moderate drinking too often turns into daily drinking or hunting for an elusive off switch. The result is consistently soaring past 1 or 2 daily drinks, repeated slips, and feeling unhealthy. Instead of struggling, some people simply opt for keeping alcohol at a distance while leaving space for the occasional glass.

Others who end up dry simply decide that moderation is too much of a hassle. The tracking, math, and effort are all too much. Rather than leave alcohol unchecked, they decide to make it a rare treat.

Another common path is to start off damp but progress to dry, almost like a graduation. In these cases, mindfulness begets mindfulness. Cutters realize they feel good when their servings are low. On top of that, they become increasingly confident they can go without alcohol—it's out of their house, they're socializing without it, and it feels less important. Eventually, being dry isn't as daunting as it once seemed and they cut to a bare minimum.

Finally, some people go dry because life told them to. Age, health, vitality, and illness are all remarkable motivators for trimming to the lowest limit. In these cases, alcohol is simply too much of a liability to be worth it. They have one here and there, but no more.

It's not uncommon for people on the dry path to take the next step and stop drinking altogether. This leads us to our last path—sobriety.

Path #5: Sober

The sober path is basically "dry" with the added emphasis of **total abstention.** No occasional drinks, no beers on the beach, no champagne at weddings—nothing. For most avid drinkers, the thought of going sober is like the end of *La La Land:* The music and dancing turns into a sad breakup. Others would sooner chew salted glass than quit entirely.

I get the resistance. Even at this point in my journey, I struggle to imagine slamming the door on alcohol. But the relationship—like my body—will continue to age. Who knows what the future holds or what diagnosis awaits?

Perceptions aside, there's a long list of great reasons for sobriety. All the reasons for going dry apply. But there's an added emphasis on **dependency issues** and **genetic predispositions.** One drink turns into two. Two turns into too many. This is why the most common path that leads to sobriety is the problematic one. If that's where your journey ends, so be it. I'll remind you one last time that there's no failure here. Just new stages.

Your Life, Your Future

My favorite thing about life is that it's full of unexpected twists and turns. I love that tomorrow isn't written yet and that we can choose to take the red pill. We can make ourselves uncomfortable enough to grow and change. And if we build a healthy environment woven through with the right habits, we're likely to thrive under any circumstance.

Drinking is one place where it's easy to opt for the blue pill. That's what I did for a long time. It was much easier to keep living in the convenient, pillow-soft world of self-assurance when it came to drinking. I imagine that was probably the case for you, too.

But then came the twist. For whatever reason, you started asking hard questions about your relationship with alcohol, just like I did. Or you at least recognized the presence of a problem that needed fixing. Either (or both) led to you to this book.

Frankly, if you had told me ten years ago that I'd write these chapters, I would've shown you my recent transactions to prove otherwise. (And asked you to reserve judgment on the Applebee's charge.) But here I am, tapping out the closing paragraphs in my home office at 5:37 AM while the women in my life slumber. This was a time of day I long associated with Vegas blackjack tables, not productivity. *That* is the power of transformation.

I hope I accomplished my goal of furnishing you with helpful tools and practical tips. More importantly, I hope those tools grow with you and help you stay damp in the long run. If you can do that, I think you'll have a great chance of finding a better version of yourself again and again. Because as great as you already are, we're all works in progress that need occasional fine-tuning.

Remember, your relationship with alcohol is alive. It changes, grows, and has birthdays. It expands and contracts. It waxes and wanes. But if we keep our mindful habits, we can stay damp for as long as it makes sense. When it stops making sense, we're free to change all over again.

Stay true to your habits, be kind to your body, and enjoy your new power over alcohol.

External Resources

There are a wide variety of alcohol issues. This being the case, *Damp* isn't the last word most drinkers will want or need to address their problem. Some will find they want more information on a specific topic. Others will be left wanting, perhaps seeking a different approach.

This section, while not exhaustive, lists a good number of external resources that might be helpful to those wanting more information.

I have broken it down into sections and included links where possible.

Literature on Moderation (Cut Lit)

- Book: *How to Change Your Drinking: A Harm Reduction Guide to Alcohol*

- Book: *Take Control of Your Drinking*, by Michael S. Levy

- Book: *The Gray Area Drinker*, by Susan Woods

- Book: *How to Be a Mindful Drinker*, by multiple authors

- Book: *Soberish*, by Kayla Lyons

- Book: *Breaking the Bottle Legacy*, by Molly J. Watts

- Book: *Mindful Drinking*, by Rosamund Dean

- Book: *Responsible Drinking*, by Frederick Rotgers et al.

- HAMS: Harm Reduction for Alcohol (https://hams.cc)

Literature on Sobriety (Quit Lit)

- Book: *Sober Curious*, by Ruby Warrington

- Book: *Alcohol Lied to Me*, by Craig Beck

- Book: *Allen Carr's Quit Drinking Without Willpower*, by Allen Carr

- Book: *Alcohol and You*, by Lewis David

- Book: *The Alcohol-Free Woman*, by Antonia Ryan and Lewis David

- Book: *This Naked Mind*, Annie Grace

- Book: *The Unexpected Joy of Being Sober*, by Catherine Gray

- Book: *Sober on a Drunk Planet*, by Sean Alexander

- Book: *Alcohol Explained*, by William Porter

Literature on Extended Breaks

- Book: *Why Can't I Drink Like Everyone Else*, by Rachel Hart

- Book: *The Alcohol Experiment*, by Annie Grace

- Book: *Try Dry*, by Dry January

- Book: *The Dry Challenge*, Hilary Sheinbaum

General Alcohol Literature

- *Drink?: The New Science of Alcohol and Health*, Professor David McNutt

Endnotes

Introduction: Welcome to a Damp Lifestyle

1. https://www.ncbi.nlm.nih.gov/pmc/articles/PMC10178867/

2. https://www.niaaa.nih.gov/publications/brochures-and-fact-sheets/understanding-alcohol-use-disorder/

3. Michael Levy (2021) *Take Control of Your Drinking*, Ch. 7

4. Frederick Rotgers, et al. (2002) *Responsible Drinking*, Ch. 1

5. https://www.ncbi.nlm.nih.gov/pmc/articles/PMC3066281/

6. https://www.rccoveryanswers.org/research-post/who-is-most-likely-to-benefit-from-moderation-focused-alcohol-treatment//

Getting Started

1. https://www.grandviewresearch.com/industry-analysis/alcoholic-drinks-market-report/

2. https://www.ncbi.nlm.nih.gov/books/NBK556005//

What Alcohol Does

1. https://www.psychologytoday.com/us/blog/the-athletes-way/201405/the-neuroscience-pleasure-and-addiction/

2. https://www.eurekalert.org/news-releases/890850/

3. https://www.ncbi.nlm.nih.gov/pmc/articles/PMC4065474/

4. https://www.ncbi.nlm.nih.gov/pmc/articles/PMC4065474/

5. For a detailed description of this process, see Chapter 2 of *Drink? The New Science of Alcohol and Health* by Professor David McNutt

6. https://pubs.niaaa.nih.gov/publications/arh294/245-255.pdf

7. https://www.webmedcentral.com/wmcpdf/Article_WMC003291.pdf

8. https://www.webmedcentral.com/wmcpdf/Article_WMC003291.pdf

9. https://pubs.niaaa.nih.gov/publications/arh27-4/285-290.htm

10. https://www.ncbi.nlm.nih.gov/pmc/articles/PMC5551541/

11. https://pubmed.ncbi.nlm.nih.gov/29889312/

Exercise 1

1. https://arcr.niaaa.nih.gov/volume/39/1/drinking-patterns-and-their-definitions/

Why We Drink, Part 1

1. https://abcnews.go.com/Business/drinking-alcohol-wine-booze-beer-work/story/

2. https://www.forbes.com/sites/allysonkapin/2020/09/15/sexual-harassment-in-silicon-valley-still-rampant-as-ever//

3. Edward Slingerland (2021) *Drunk*, Ch. 2

4. https://www.sciencedirect.com/science/article/abs/pii/S1053810012000037

5. https://www.ncbi.nlm.nih.gov/pmc/articles/PMC5700800/

6. Michael Andrews (2020) Bar Talk: Informal Social Interactions, Alcohol Prohibition, and Invention. https://economics.harvard.edu/files/economics/files/bar_talk_3_20.pdf

7. Robert Putnam's *Bowling Alone* is a good example of this literature.

8. https://www.eandvgroup.com/the-cocktail-napkin-hall-of-fame/

9. https://www.forbes.com/forbes/2009/0216o%20/026/

10. https://read.oecd-ilibrary.org/social-issues-migration-health/tackling-harmful-alcohol-use_9789264181069-en/

11. https://www.sciencedirect.com/science/article/abs/pii/S0306460314001683/

12. https://psycnet.apa.org/record/2011-16179-003/

13. https://www.nbcnews.com/id/wbna48722340/

14. https://asia.nikkei.com/Spotlight/Society/China-s-business-drinking-culture-spurs-MeToo-moment/

15. Edward Slingerland (2021) *Drunk*, Ch. 3

Why We Drink, Part 2

1. https://news.gallup.com/poll/473057/loneliness-subsides-pandemic-high.aspx

2. https://legacy.cigna.com/static/www-cigna-com/docs/about-us/newsroom/studies-and-reports/combatting-loneliness/cigna-2020-loneliness-report.pdf

3. https://www.aarp.org/content/dam/aarp/ppi/2017/10/medicare-spends-more-on-socially-isolated-older-adults.pdf

4. https://www.vivekmurthy.com/post/2017/10/10/work-and-the-loneliness-epidemic-harvard-business-review

5. https://www.health.harvard.edu/blog/this-is-your-brain-on-alcohol-2017071412000

6. https://www.psychologicalscience.org/news/releases/moderate-doses-of-alcohol-increase-social-bonding-in-groups.html

7. https://www.researchgate.net/publication/44614057/

8. https://www.researchgate.net/publication/7906448/

9. https://pubmed.ncbi.nlm.nih.gov/27936361/

10. https://pubmed.ncbi.nlm.nih.gov/32104646/

11. https://www.businessinsider.com/japanese-government-dating-services-2016-10/

12. Aziz Ansari (2015) *Modern Romance*, Ch. 5

13. https://www.chinadaily.com.cn/a/202103/23/WS605956e3a31024ad0bab0f39.html

14. https://www.businessinsider.com/tokyo-funds-matchmaking-parties-to-boost-japans-birth-rates-2014-3/

15. https://www.nippon.com/en/japan-data/h01128/

16. https://alcohol.org/guides/drinking-on-dates/

17. https://pubmed.ncbi.nlm.nih.gov/1091942/

18. https://www.glamour.com/story/first-dates-lead-to-marriage/

19. https://www.sciencedaily.com/releases/2015/05/150519210251.htm/

20. https://www.health.harvard.edu/mind-and-mood/oxytocin-the-love-hormone/

21. https://onlinelibrary.wiley.com/doi/abs/10.1111/pere.12115

22. https://www.ncbi.nlm.nih.gov/pmc/articles/PMC1647300/

23. https://academic.oup.com/psychsocgerontology/article/73/4/655/2631996

24. https://www.ncbi.nlm.nih.gov/pmc/articles/PMC6811721/

25. https://www.ncbi.nlm.nih.gov/pmc/articles/PMC1647300/

26. https://www.sciencedirect.com/science/article/abs/pii/S2352250X16300677

27. https://www.psychologytoday.com/us/blog/all-about-sex/201907/the-pros-and-cons-mixing-sex-and-alcohol/

28. https://www.cancer.org/latest-news/the-study-that-helped-spur-the-us-stop-smoking-movement.html

29. https://truthinitiative.org/press/press-release/big-tobacco-finally-forced-tell-truth-about-its-deadly-products-through-court/

30. https://www.lshtm.ac.uk/newsevents/news/2018/alcohol-industry-misleading-public-about-alcohol-related-cancer-risk/

31. https://winefolly.com/lifestyle/wine-sex-drive-match/

32. https://www.thelancet.com/journals/unidentified_journal/article/PII0140-6736(92)91277 -F/fulltext

33. https://www.ncbi.nlm.nih.gov/pmc/articles/PMC5513687/

34. https://www.thelancet.com/article/S0140-6736(18)31571-X/fulltext

35. See, for example, https://www.thespiritsbusiness.com/2019/06/analysis-uncovering-que stionable-alcohol-studies// , https://www.thedrinksbusiness.com/2021/10/flaw-found-in -no-safe-level-of-drinking-claim// , and https://www.thespiritsbusiness.com/2019/05/tra de-hits-out-at-questionable-lancet-alcohol-research// .

36. https://www.parkinsons.org.uk/news/people-who-smoke-may-be-less-likely-develop-pa rkinsons/

Why We Should Cut Back

1. https://www.washingtonpost.com/news/wonk/wp/2015/02/09/how-just-a-couple-drinks -make-your-odds-of-a-car-crash-skyrocket

2. https://www.alcoholrehabguide.org/resources/medical-conditions/injury/

3. https://www.cancer.gov/about-cancer/causes-prevention/risk/alcohol/alcohol-fact-sheet

4. https://www.cancer.org/cancer/esophagus-cancer/about/what-is-cancer-of-the-esophag us.html

5. https://www.nature.com/articles/bjc2014579.pdf

6. https://seer.cancer.gov/statfacts/html/esoph.html

7. https://www.nature.com/articles/bjc2014579.pdf

8. https://pubmed.ncbi.nlm.nih.gov/21307158//

9. https://www.nature.com/articles/s41598-018-26856-w

10. https://www.niehs.nih.gov/health/topics/conditions/breast-cancer/index.cfm/

11. https://seer.cancer.gov/statfacts/html/breast.html/

12. https://www.verywellhealth.com/estrogen-suppression-and-role-womens-health-430138 /

13. https://www.cancer.org/cancer/breast-cancer/understanding-a-breast-cancer-diagnosis/b reast-cancer-hormone-receptor-status.html

14. https://pubs.niaaa.nih.gov/publications/arh22-3/220.pdf

208

15. https://journals.sagepub.com/doi/10.2217/WHE.14.62

16. https://www.nature.com/articles/bjc2014579.pdf

17. https://link.springer.com/article/10.1007%2Fs12609-013-0114-z

18. https://journals.sagepub.com/doi/10.2217/WHE.14.62

19. https://seer.cancer.gov/statfacts/html/breast.html

20. https://www.webmd.com/heart-disease/heart-disease-alcohol-your-heart/

21. https://www.heartandstroke.ca/articles/ask-a-cardiologist-alcohol-and-heart-health/

22. https://www.ncbi.nlm.nih.gov/pmc/articles/PMC5513687/

23. William Porter (2015) *Alcohol Explained*, Ch. 6

24. https://pubs.niaaa.nih.gov/publications/AA85/AA85.htm/

25. https://www.webmd.com/depression/alcohol-and-depression/

26. https://www.health.com/weight-loss/does-alcohol-make-you-gain-weight/

27. https://www.insider.com/guides/health/diet-nutrition/does-alcohol-make-you-gain-weight/

28. https://medlineplus.gov/ency/patientinstructions/000886.htm/

29. https://www.betterhealth.vic.gov.au/health/healthyliving/Alcohol-and-weight-gain/

30. https://www.hsph.harvard.edu/obesity-prevention-source/obesity-causes/sleep-and-obesity/

31. https://www.ncbi.nlm.nih.gov/pmc/articles/PMC4338356/

32. https://www.nbcnews.com/health/body-odd/hangovers-really-do-get-worse-we-get-older-heres-why-n1981/

33. https://www.nature.com/articles/bjc2014579.pdf

34. https://onlinelibrary.wiley.com/doi/10.1002/ijc.33538

Why Mindfulness Works

1. https://www.ncbi.nlm.nih.gov/pmc/articles/PMC5737497/

2. https://www.ncbi.nlm.nih.gov/pmc/articles/PMC4489711/

3. https://www.ncbi.nlm.nih.gov/pmc/articles/PMC3004979/

4. https://pubmed.ncbi.nlm.nih.gov/34335292/

5. https://pubmed.ncbi.nlm.nih.gov/30525995//

The Importance of Motivation

1. Levy, Michael (2021) *Take Control of Your Drinking*, Ch. 4

2. https://alcohol.org/guides/drinking-on-dates/

Exercise 3

1. Stephen Guise (2013), *Mini Habits*.

Understanding Alcohol Habits

1. https://www.tandfonline.com/doi/full/10.1080/14681360500487470

2. https://www.psychologytoday.com/us/blog/your-personal-renaissance/202010/5-ways-break-your-bad-habit-now/

3. https://www.psychologytoday.com/us/blog/the-winner-effect/201301/brain-vacations-stress-boredom-and-travel/

4. James Clear (2018) *Atomic Habits*, Ch. 3

5. James Clear (2018) *Atomic Habits*, Ch. 3

6. https://coloradosun.com/2018/12/11/colorado-beer-new-law-2019/

7. https://www.thedenverchannel.com/news/360/common-consumption-could-be-on-tap-as-early-as-this-summer-in-denver

8. https://www.usatoday.com/story/news/nation/2013/02/01/dry-towns-alcohol-bans-blue-laws/1884513/

9. https://247wallst.com/special-report/2019/12/12/states-that-still-have-dry-counties/3/

10. See https://www.npr.org/sections/thetwo-way/2017/07/02/535259524/utahs-zion-curtain-falls-and-loosens-states-tight-liquor-laws and https://www.sltrib.com/news/2019/06/15/things-expect-when-utah/

11. https://www.delish.com/food-news/a50802/disney-magic-kingdom-drinking-rules/

12. https://www.nytimes.com/2013/02/24/magazine/the-extraordinary-science-of-junk-food.html

13. https://www.mashed.com/220445/nutritionist-explains-why-cheetos-are-so-addictive/

14. https://www.nytimes.com/2013/02/24/magazine/the-extraordinary-science-of-junk-food.html

15. https://www.fastcompany.com/1769238/neurofocus-uses-neuromarketing-hack-your-brain/

16. https://thearf.org/2009-arf-david-ogilvy-awards-winners//

Interlude

1. https://www.acpjournals.org/doi/10.7326/M20-7271

2. https://nielseniq.com/global/en/insights/analysis/2020/rebalancing-the-covid-19-effect-on-alcohol-sales/

3. https://www.acpjournals.org/doi/10.7326/M20-7271

4. Kenneth Anderson (2010) *How to Change Your Drinking*, Ch. 15

Counting Alcohol Servings

1. https://www.rethinkingdrinking.niaaa.nih.gov/How-much-is-too-much/What-counts-as-a-drink/Whats-A-Standard-Drink.aspx

2. In the formula, ounces per serving is calculated by dividing the number of ounces in a standard serving by the alcohol by volume (ABV). The 60 in the formula comes from the number of fluid ounces that are in a standard alcohol serving (0.6). Keep in mind that ABV is a percentage, so a 5% ABV is actually 0.05 if expressed in number form. So the original formula for a 5% ABV beer would have been 0.6 ÷ 0.05 = 12 ouncer per serving. All I did was simplify the math by multiplying everything by 100 (60 ÷ 5% ABV = 12 ounces per serving).

Creating Your Drinking Goals

1. https://www.cdc.gov/nchs/nhis/alcohol/alcohol_glossary.htm/

2. https://www.niaaa.nih.gov/alcohol-health/overview-alcohol-consumption/moderate-binge-drinking/

3. https://arcr.niaaa.nih.gov/volume/39/1/drinking-patterns-and-their-definitions/

4. Levy, Michael (2021) *Taking Control of Your Drinking*, Ch. 9

5. Interview with Dax Shephard on Armchair Expert podcast.

6. https://www.aeaweb.org/articles?id=10.1257/app.20130327/

Setting Up Your Environment

1. https://www.axios.com/2017/12/15/sean-parker-unloads-on-facebook-god-only-knows-what-its-doing-to-our-childrens-brains-1513306792/

2. https://www.reviews.org/mobile/cell-phone-addiction/

3. https://www.businessinsider.com/facebook-has-been-deliberately-designed-to-mimic-addictive-painkillers-2018-12/

4. https://www.healthline.com/health/alcohol-cravings/

Practical Tips for Moderation

1. https://sites.duke.edu/apep/module-1-gender-matters/content/content-how-is-alcohol-absorbed-into-the-body/

2. . https://www.health.com/condition/type-2-diabetes/why-sugar-makes-you-thirsty/

3. https://www.healthline.com/nutrition/best-foods-to-eat-before-drinking/

4. https://www.nature.com/articles/npp201391/

Street Smarts

1. https://www.thedailybeast.com/the-newest-trend-in-bars-no-booze/

2. https://bmcpublichealth.biomedcentral.com/articles/10.1186/s12889-020-09060-2/

3. https://www.drinkaware.co.uk/news/new-research-lifts-lid-on-peer-pressure-culture-around-alcohol/

Supporting Your Mindful Habits

1. James Clear (2018) *Atomic Habits*, Ch. 2

2. https://journals.lww.com/addictiondisorders/Abstract/2021/12000/Effectiveness_of_the_Cognitive_Restructuring.13.aspx

3. https://www.psychologytoday.com/us/blog/automatic-you/202206/the-key-behavior-change-is-identity-change

4. https://iaap-journals.onlinelibrary.wiley.com/doi/10.1111/aphw.12120

5. For more on this, see Frederick Rotgers et al. (2002) *Responsible Drinking*, Ch. 9.

Be Ready for Slips and Setbacks

1. https://www.ncbi.nlm.nih.gov/pmc/articles/PMC7763183/

2. https://link.springer.com/referenceworkentry/10.1007/978-1-4419-1005-9_1496/

3. https://www.ncbi.nlm.nih.gov/pmc/articles/PMC4695236//

The Value of Extended Breaks

1. https://www.vice.com/en/article/5gjakb/how-much-of-a-nightmare-is-dry-january-for-british-pubs-off-licences-restaurants-203

2. https://www.ncbi.nlm.nih.gov/pmc/articles/PMC5942469/

3. https://pubmed.ncbi.nlm.nih.gov/26690637/

4. https://joinclubsoda.com/hub/moderate-drinking-successful//

Looking Forward: The New You

1. Frederick Rotgers et al. (2002) *Responsible Drinking*, Chapter 12